THE
Archive Photographs
SERIES

VICKERS AIRCRAFT

SPANNING THE DECADES. The Royal Air Force Vickers VC10 C. Mk.1 strategic multi-mission jet transport at the time of the first delivery to RAF Transport Command in July 1966, seen through the rigging of the splendid flying replica of its original Vickers military aircraft predecessor, the First World War Vickers Gunbus biplane fighter, which was built by the Vintage Aircraft and Flying Association (VAFA) at Weybridge that same year to commemorate the centenary of the Royal Aeronautical Society (itself formed a year before Vickers Sons and Company was formed for steel-making in Sheffield). The original Vickers Gunbus was the world's first aircraft specifically designed to mount a machine gun. The Vickers VC10 was the largest aircraft ever to go into series production in Britain. While the VC10 is expected to continue in front-line global service with the RAF in strategic transport and aerial refuelling tanker roles well into the next millennium, the Vickers Gunbus replica has for the last thirty years been proudly displayed in the RAF Museum at Hendon, North London. Together these two famous Vickers aircraft types effectively span the entire spectrum of world-leading aviation technology created and developed by Vickers; they characterise the extraordinary story illustrated in the following pages.

THE
Archive Photographs
SERIES

VICKERS AIRCRAFT

Compiled by
Norman Barfield

CHALFORD

First published 1997
Copyright © Norman Barfield, 1997

The Chalford Publishing Company
St Mary's Mill, Chalford,
Stroud, Gloucestershire, GL6 8NX

ISBN 0 7524 0606 X

Typesetting and origination by
The Chalford Publishing Company
Printed in Great Britain by
Redwood Books, Trowbridge

Dedicated to
Sir George Edwards
who steered so much of the great Vickers aviation enterprise with
commanding vision, courage, conviction and compassion

Cover Illustration. Final assembly of the ubiquitous Vickers Wellington twin-engined bomber at Smith's Lawn in Windsor Great Park during the Second World War – one of nearly ninety manufacturing dispersal sites rapidly set up in the local area following the disastrous bombing of the main Vickers factory at Weybridge in September 1940. Augmented by the huge government-owned Shadow Factories at Chester and Blackpool in the North of England, the extremely complex, high-rate, production programme for the Wellington produced a grand total of 11,461 aircraft built between 1938 and 1945. In wartime service, this most distinctive Vickers' aircraft type bore the brunt of the RAF bomber offensive against Germany until the advent of the four-engined heavies, and went on to serve in every Command of the Royal Air Force, except Fighter, before becoming a pioneering engine testbed aircraft prefacing Vickers bold entry into the post-war jet age. The Vickers Wellington can therefore be regarded as one of the most successful British aircraft programmes ever.

Contents

The Vickers Aviation Siblings

Vickers first evinced interest in aviation in July 1908 when the Admiralty asked the company to construct a Zeppelin-type airship, Britain's first. During the ensuing seventy years this illustrious British engineering company then engaged in five distinct lines of aviation activity: airships, aircraft, founding the British aviation equipment accessories industry, founding the Canadian aviation industry, and the acquisition of Supermarine. Between 1908 and 1929, the company designed and built a series of rigid- and non-rigid airships culminating in the trans-Atlantic R.100, Britain's last in view of the horrendous loss of the government-built R.101 in October 1930.

Aircraft construction was begun in 1911 at Erith, Kent, and a flying school established the following year at Brooklands, near Weybridge in Surrey, the scene of much of the early British pioneering effort in aviation. Contracted by the War Office and Admiralty to build numerous other types during the First World War, from 1915 Vickers began to concentrate its aircraft activities at Weybridge.

Canadian Vickers, originally established as a general engineering and shipbuilding enterprise in Montreal in 1911, also formed an aviation division in 1922, thus laying the foundation of the Canadian aircraft industry. During the subsequent twenty-two years, this Canadian aviation arm not only built types emanating from the two parent Vickers' aviation units (Weybridge and Supermarine) but also those of its own conception, as well as large numbers of many types under licence from other British, Dutch and American aircraft companies during the Second World War, before being transferred to the Crown company, Canadair, in 1944.

A merger of the heavy engineering interests of Vickers and Armstrong Whitworth in 1928 resulted in a new company known as Vickers-Armstrongs Limited. Vickers (Aviation) Limited was formed to take over the Aviation Department. (However, Sir W.G. Armstrong Whitworth Aircraft Ltd was not included in this merger and later became part of the rival Hawker Siddeley Group). Significantly, this was also the year in which Supermarine*, the highly-accomplished seaplane specialist founded in 1913 and inspired by the brilliant Reginald Mitchell, was acquired by Vickers and was thereafter officially known as the Supermarine Aviation Works (Vickers) Limited.

Although Supermarine continued to operate with almost total autonomy below board level in parallel with its parent company, the Weybridge-based Vickers (Aviation) Ltd, in 1938 both units were taken over by Vickers-Armstrongs Ltd. After massive output of the Wellington bomber and Spitfire fighter during the Second World War, including production at the huge government-owned Shadow Factories at Chester and Blackpool; Castle Bromwich, near Birmingham and South Marston, near Swindon, respectively, by the early 1960s the aircraft elements of Supermarine had finally been absorbed into what had by then become Vickers-Armstrongs (Aircraft) Ltd at Weybridge (which since 1951 had also operated a major satellite factory at Hurn (Bournemouth) Airport) – until it, too, became one of the three partners in British Aircraft Corporation (BAC) on its formation in 1960. The Vickers name disappeared from the visible masthead of British aviation with the consolidation of the BAC organisation in 1964 – although Vickers Ltd continued as a 40 (and later 50) per cent shareholder in the new merged company. With the nationalisation of the UK aircraft industry in 1977, BAC then became part of the (later privatised) British Aerospace PLC which was 'vested' on 29 April 1977 and officially constituted on 1 January 1978. Hence Vickers prime involvement in aviation finally ceased only a few months short of seventy years from its bold beginning in July 1908.

Although Vickers PLC continues to produce an important range of aerospace products, its main business today lies in the automotive, defence systems, propulsion technology and medical equipment fields. Nevertheless, both Vickers and British Aerospace continue to be proud to count these pioneering and historic Vickers aviation siblings among their original illustrious predecessors.

* The subject of a separate volume in *The Archive Photographs Series*.

Introduction

Vickers, one of Britain's longest-established and most widely-accomplished engineering companies, played a leading role in the development of aviation for almost seventy years – realising an unequalled range of aeronautical business, technological, operational, record-breaking and prize-winning achievements, and British and world 'firsts'. In its early years in the aviation business, Vickers also laid the foundations of the British aircraft equipment accessories industry, the Canadian aircraft industry, and acquired Supermarine, the world-renowned seaplane specialist of Southampton.

Forceful management, combined with brilliant design and imaginative production, carried the Vickers aviation aspirations from the provision of Britain's first airships and teaching some of its earliest aviators to fly, on through a rich cavalcade of almost every type of aircraft, through the triumphs and traumas of its massive contributions to the winning of two World Wars, to an outstanding post-war jet-age family. This began with Britain's first post-war airliner and culminated in the VC10, the largest aircraft type ever to go into series production in Britain. As a primary shareholder in the British Aircraft Corporation (an immediate predecessor of today's British Aerospace), Vickers also had a major share of the Anglo-French Concorde programme.

A Vickers VC10 rear-engined intercontinental jet airliner for British Overseas Airways Corporation (BOAC) taking off from the 3,750 ft runway at Brooklands, where it was designed and built, and thus demonstrating its impressive short-field performance in Vickers own backyard before landing at the company's flight test airfield at Wisley, three miles to the south of the Weybridge factory. The VC10 and Super VC10 continue to serve with the RAF in the vital strategic transport and aerial tanker roles.

Genesis

Unlike most of the other great early British aircraft manufacturing companies, Vickers did not take its name from an aviation pioneer signatory but from a firm with a long history in steel-making, shipbuilding and armaments, which early recognised the military potential of aviation. Tracing the Vickers family business origins from as far back as the 1750s, Vickers Sons and Company was incorporated in Sheffield in the steel-making business in 1867. Just thirty years later, and now a hundred years ago, the company became known as Vickers Sons and Maxim Limited when, in 1897, it acquired Maxim Nordenfelt Guns and Ammunition Co. Ltd whereby the original Maxim machine-gun was subsequently developed into the famous Vickers gun that became widely used in military aircraft. Hiram Maxim, an ex-patriate American, was an aeronautical pioneer before his association with Vickers, having built a large and ungainly steam-powered structure in Kent in 1894 which cost him more than £20,000 but which was unsuccessful. Nevertheless, he later became a British citizen and was knighted.

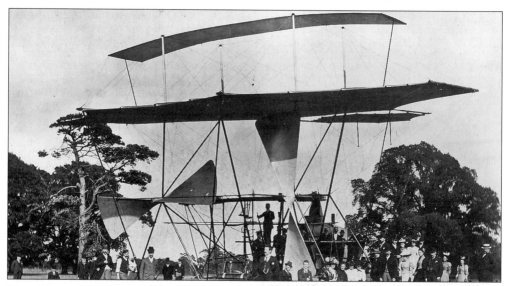

Hiram Maxim's massive but uncontrollable flying machine at Baldwyn's Park, Bexley, Kent, in July 1894, shortly before it crashed. With five sets of wings, the three centre pairs could be removed to vary the wing area from 5,400 sq ft to 4,000 sq ft. (Compare that to the 2,932 sq ft for the Vickers VC10 seven decades later). With a total weight of 4,000 lb it was powered by two compound steam engines delivering 363 hp each, driving a propeller of 17 ft 10 in diameter at 375 rpm. The overall span was 125 ft and the length was 104 ft – about two-thirds the scale of the modern VC10.

Airships: Britain's First to Last

Vickers first showed interest in aviation in its own right in 1908, less than five years after the American Wright brothers had made the world's first powered man-carrying flights in December 1903. On 21 July 1908 the company submitted a proposal at the invitation of the Admiralty to construct a large rigid airship, the first in Britain, in response to the evident success achieved in this field by Count von Zeppelin in Germany. Officially named HMA (His Majesty's Airship) No.1, and optimistically nicknamed 'Mayfly', although it did incorporate some bold innovations, the scant structural knowledge then available meant that this first foray into aviation was not successful – it suffered structural failure when emerging from its shed at the Vickers' shipyard at Barrow-in-Furness in 1911. Nevertheless, during the protracted design period, Vickers had obtained all proprietary rights in the German-invented aluminium-based light alloy, duralumin, which promoted a major increase in strength in airframe structures and has been the primary material for aircraft construction ever since.

Britain's first airship, the Vickers HMA 1 ('Mayfly') which was initiated in 1908 as the company's first venture into the fledgling aeronautical business and completed in 1911 at Cavendish Dock in the Vickers shipbuilding facility at Barrow-in-Furness. However, disaster struck in the form of a sudden gust of wind which broke it up as it emerged from its shed on 24 September 1911. The Vickers R.9, which followed in 1916, was the first British rigid airship to fly successfully; the Vickers R100 of 1929 was the last.

Early Vickers monoplanes, built at Erith, Kent, serving the Vickers' Flying School established in 1912 within the world's first closed-circuit, banked, motor racing track at Brooklands near Weybridge, and dubbed 'The Birthplace of British Motorsport and Aviation'. Vickers' aircraft sheds Nos 37, 38, 39 and 40 near the Byfleet banking were part of the Brooklands Aviation Village that was so graphically depicted in the comic film *Those Magnificent Men in their Flying Machines*.

Disbanded for two years, the Vickers' airship department was reconstituted in 1913 to design and build HMA No.9 under Hartley Pratt who had been engaged from S.E. Saunders of Cowes, Isle of Wight, after being critical of the Mayfly. He brought with him a youthful Barnes Wallis, who had been apprenticed to the shipbuilders J. Samuel White, also of Cowes. Wallis soon became the dominant designer and Vickers went on to design and build a total of six rigid and three non-rigid airships plus a number of SS (Sea Scout) 'Blimps' at its shipbuilding yard at Barrow-in-Furness, culminating in the trans-Atlantic R.100 airship built at Howden in

The superb Weybridge-based Vintage Aircraft and Flying Association (VAFA) flying replica of the Vickers Gunbus fighting biplane of First World War fame which was widely flown and displayed in 1966, including inspection by the Queen at Abingdon, Oxfordshire, before being permanently preserved for public appreciation at the RAF Museum, Hendon, North London.

Yorkshire, for which the Vickers' subsidiary, the Airship Guarantee Company, was specially formed with Wallis as its Chief Engineer. As it turned out, the R.100 proved to be the last before the British airship programme was abruptly terminated following the horrendous crash of the government-built R.101 airship at Beauvais, Northern France, in October 1930. This was the beginning of Wallis's fifty-eight year association with Vickers which eventually spanned four separate careers – airships, the geodetic bomber generation of the 1930s and 40s, his 'Dambusting' and other key weapons of the Second World War and, finally, his visionary projections for future global communications when Head of the Vickers Aeronautical Research and Development Department at Weybridge in the post-war years until his retirement in 1971 at the age of 84.

Early Monoplanes and Fighting Biplanes

Despite the failure of the first Vickers airship in 1911, the company was not deterred and, adopting the shortened title of Vickers Limited, established an aircraft manufacturing capability during that same year at its engineering works at Erith. It built a series of braced monoplanes, based on an original French design, which were used by the flying school set up at Brooklands, near Weybridge, a year later. Contracted by the War Office to build large numbers of various government-designed aircraft types during the First Word War at Erith, Crayford and Bexleyeath, in 1915 Vickers began to concentrate its aircraft activity in the former Itala motor works at Brooklands, by then Britain's primary aviation centre. The Vickers aircraft design team, hitherto based at Imperial Court in London's Knightsbridge, also moved there in 1919.

The first aircraft type produced by Vickers at Weybridge was the BE2c biplane designed at the Royal Aircraft Factory at Farnborough, of which 75 were made at a cost of £975 each. Fifty Farnborough-designed FE8 biplanes were also built at Weybridge in 1916, followed by 1,650 SE5a biplane fighters specifically designed to combat the German Zeppelin airship threat, by far the largest share of the overall wartime SE5a production programme. The first indigenous Vickers' design to go into production there was the FB9 Gunbus. The Gunbus was the world's first aircraft designed to mount a machine-gun. Also built in France, the Gunbus was successfully deployed during the early part of the war.

For the next thirty years, until the late 1940s and the advent of the Vickers Viscount, the world's first turbine-powered airliner to enter service, the Vickers' design team was brilliantly led by Rex Pierson, whose first major achievement was the famous Vickers Vimy bomber in 1917 when he was made Chief Designer at the age of only 26.

Founding the Aircraft Equipment Industry

It was also at this time that Vickers began to develop a large range of specialised aircraft equipment accessories and became bulk suppliers to the rest of the British aircraft industry and to overseas customers. Tommy Duncan led much of this effort and was responsible for the first British patented oleo-pneumatic landing gear shock-absorbers. The Vickers range also included fuel pumps and cocks, Vickers-Potts oil coolers, Vickers-Reid blind-flying instruments, Vickers-Davis navigation lights and a host of VGS (Vickers General Stores) parts in addition to AGS (Aircraft General Stores) common fittings which became standardised from the First World War. It was from this vital branch of the Vickers early aviation activity that much of the aircraft ancillary equipment industry of today is descended. Although having to drop much of this enterprise when substantial aircraft orders began to flow into the company under the Royal Air Force expansion scheme of 1935, the capability to design and manufacture complete landing gears was retained right through to that for the Vickers VC10 jetliner of the 1960s.

The Pioneering Vimy and the Bomber-Transports

A special adaptation of the Vickers Vimy triumphantly established the first non-stop, trans-Atlantic and others the first England-to-Australia and England-to-Southern Africa aerial links in 1919/20, thereby opening up what are among the key intercontinental airlanes of the world as we know them today and winning substantial and prestigious monetary prizes in the process. From the Vimy stemmed an impressive lineage of large military biplane bomber-transports: Vernon, Virginia, Victoria and Valentia, that formed the backbone of this capability during the formative years of the Royal Air Force. Additionally, the cabin-type (eight-seat) Vimy Commercial of 1922, which operated the first regular London-to-Paris air service, was justifiably dubbed 'The Father of the Airliner'.

A defining moment in British and world aviation: the Vickers Vimy, powered by Rolls-Royce Eagle engines, taking off from Newfoundland in 1919 at the beginning of its pioneering first direct non-stop flight across the Atlantic to Southern Ireland in the hands of Alcock and Brown. Other Vimys quickly followed this triumph with the first flights from England to Australia and to Southern Africa, thereby opening up the key intercontinental commercial airlanes that we know today.

The Inter-War Intermediaries

Complementing its primary bomber-transport family, Vickers also engaged in a wide range of intermediate aircraft types during the inter-war years before, and alongside, the emergence of its famous 'geodetic generation' and won a world height record in 1932. These types included amphibians, light competition aircraft, biplane scouts, biplane and monoplane transports, general purpose and torpedo bomber biplanes and monoplane fighters, prefacing the wholesale swing to the monoplane era in the 1930s and the preparation for the large-scale requirements of the impending European conflict.

Canadian Vickers

A significant extension of Vickers' aviation interests was also made in 1922 when Canadian Vickers, at the invitation of the Canadian Government, formed an aviation division in Montreal – so laying the foundation of the Canadian aircraft industry. Beginning with a contract to build eight Vickers-Weybridge designed Viking amphibians, this Canadian air arm built a range of aircraft types of its own conception specifically for Canadian regional development, as well as large numbers of many types under licence from Vickers-Supermarine and other British, Dutch and American aircraft companies, notably during the Second World War. In 1941, Canadian Vickers moved its aircraft activities to a government factory at Cartierville before being transferred to the Crown company Canadair Ltd in 1944, which later became a subsidiary of the American General Dynamics Corporation.

The Geodetic Generation

The advent of the monoplane era at Weybridge in the 1930s under the bold management direction of Sir Robert McLean and the design direction of Rex Pierson – via the Barnes Wallis-devised geodetic ('basketweave') structural principle initially realised in the Vickers Wellesley monoplane bomber – was the next really significant step in the Vickers-Weybridge aircraft dynasty. The outstanding success of this uniquely-distinctive aircraft generation was highlighted by the world-record long-distance flight by Vickers Wellesleys from Egypt to Australia in 1938 followed by the production of more than 12,000 Vickers Wellington and Warwick bombers during the Second World War.

The Vickers' aviation factory on the east side of the Brooklands site during the inter-war years, with the huge company name immediately adjacent to the world-famous motor racing track, grandstand and finishing straight, providing the kind of advertising hoarding so sought after at modern aviation and motorsport venues.

The Shadows and Dispersals of War

Nationwide factory dispersal was obviously imperative to handle such a large, high-rate, wartime production volume and was also made necessary following the devastating German bombing raid on the Vickers aircraft factory at Brooklands in September 1940. Wellington production was immediately dispersed to nearly ninety local locations including motor garages, film studios and the Woolworths store in Weybridge town centre. With a spirit that was characteristic, full-scale production was quickly resumed at the Weybridge plant and, with the continued support of these outstations, 2,514 Wellingtons were completed there – about a fifth of the total national output of this quite remarkable aircraft. The entire complement of 845 of the Wellington's bigger sibling, the Warwick, was also produced at Weybridge in the latter stages of the war. The huge government-owned Shadow Factories at Broughton, near Chester, and at Squire's Gate, near Blackpool, each with their own satellites, also produced another 5,540 and 3,406 Wellingtons respectively. The national output of this versatile aircraft thus totalled 11,461 units between 1938 and 1945. The Wellington was Britain's most numerous and successful two-motor bomber of the Second World War. It bore the brunt of the bomber offensive during the early part of the war until the advent of the four-engined heavies and served in every Command of the Royal Air Force, except Fighter.

The Post-War Progression – Britain's First to Biggest

Despite the extreme rigours and exigencies of war, the Vickers' team at Weybridge was quick off the mark immediately after the cessation of hostilities in Europe with a bold foray into the civil aircraft field. The first flight of the Vickers Viking VC1 (Vickers Commercial One), a civil adaptation of the Wellington, was made on 22 June 1945, only six weeks after VE Day, making it Britain's first post-war airliner.

The interim Viking formed the backbone of the newly-formed British European Airways (BEA) fleet from its formation in 1946 and through its formative years. It also sold well in many other parts of the world and was chosen to reactivate the King's Flight with a royal tour of South Africa in 1947. The experimental Rolls-Royce Nene pure jet-powered Vickers Viking of 1948 was the world's first civil transport aircraft to be powered exclusively by jet propulsion and

The Weybridge-built Vickers Wellington 'R for Robert' N2980 that was dramatically rescued from Loch Ness in September 1985, after ditching there following engine failure in a blizzard during a navigational training flight from Lossiemouth on New Year's Eve 1940 and which has since been painstakingly restored at Brooklands Museum. Clearly exhibiting the characteristic Barnes Wallis devised geodetic ('basketweave') structure, this is the only surviving Wellington to have seen active service during the Second World War. The only other Wellington extant is the post-war trainer at the RAF Museum.

One of the sixty Vickers Viscount Type 745D turboprop airliners ordered in 1955 by Capital Airlines of the USA which constituted Britain's largest single dollar export in any field up to that time. The Viscount was the world's first turbine-powered airliner to enter commercial service in 1950, and went on to pioneer turbine-powered flight throughout the world with sales totalling 438 aircraft. Two hundred and seventy-nine of these were built at the Vickers satellite factory at Hurn (Bournemouth) Airport, which was established in 1951 (initially building most of Vickers Varsity military transports) to ease the burgeoning Vickers production volume at Weybridge.

established a long-standing speed record between London and Paris. The Viking thus became the harbinger of a family progression of large jet-age civil and military aircraft realised by the Vickers-Weybridge team in the succeeding twenty years, under the astute and commanding leadership of the indomitable (later Sir) George Edwards, that was unique in the Western World and ranged from Britain's first to biggest.

From the Viking followed two significant military derivatives – the mutli-role Valetta, the first post-war transport developed for the Royal Air Force, and the Varsity, the RAF's long-serving multi-engined transport aircraft flight and navigational crew trainer. The Vickers Viscount, initially conceived by Rex Pierson before his untimely death in 1948, and spurred by his successor, George Edwards, pioneered the benefits of turbine-powered air transport throughout the world. Edwards also succeeded Sir Hew Kilner, the indefatigable Vickers' aviation leader during the Second World War on his death at the age of only 61 in 1953.

Then came the Valiant, first of the RAF's much-vaunted V-bomber force, conceived by Edwards and driven through to service in record time in his characteristically resolute style. The Vanguard followed, a large, low-cost propeller-turbine transport which ushered in large-scale airframe structural machining and a new airframe anti-corrosion protection process at Weybridge. Developed in the 1960s were the VC10 and Super VC10 rear-engined intercontinental jetliners, Britain's largest-ever aircraft to enter series production and of which more than half the weight of the airframe was machined from the solid.

The ill-fated TSR2 supersonic bomber conceived in the late 1950s was the catalyst for the formation of the British Aircraft Corporation (BAC) by government dictum in 1960. The two principal parent companies, Vickers Ltd and English Electric Ltd, each held 40 (later 50) per cent shareholdings in the new company which were physically vested in their aviation subsidiaries Vickers-Armstrongs (Aircraft) Ltd at Weybridge and English Electric Aviation Ltd of Preston, Lancashire, which were contracted to design and build the TSR2 in equal partnership. Paradoxically, after continuing to be known by these names for the next four years, the government cancellation of the TSR2 programme in 1965 was again the catalyst whereby both these long-established British aviation companies finally lost their visible identities with the consolidation of the BAC organisation, headquartered at Weybridge.

Under the unifying chairmanship of the heroic Royal Air Force wartime leader, Lord Portal, in partnership with Sir George Edwards, first as Executive Director-Aircraft and later as managing director, the new group soon gave birth to the BAC One-Eleven, the world's first tailored-for-the-job short-haul jetliner. This was developed by the Weybridge team from the imaginative Hunting H107 project which came into the BAC fold with the acquisition of that company's air arm at Luton, Bedfordshire. The BAC One-Eleven was largely built at the Hurn (Bournemouth) plant which, for a period during the Viscount programme, had been the world's

One of the thirty BAC One-Eleven twin jet airliners bought by America Airlines in the mid 1960s. The world's first specifically 'tailored for the job' domestic and regional jet airliner, the BAC One-Eleven won major orders for Britain before the arrival of American domestic equivalents. More than two-thirds of the total sales of 232 aircraft were for export.

most productive turbine-powered airliner factory. Both types made major inroads into the tough American domestic market ahead of 'home-grown' equivalents.

Simultaneously, the Weybridge team was entrusted with a major share of the Anglo-French (British Aircraft Corporation – Sud Aviation) Concorde supersonic airliner programme, for which it made the largest single contribution in design, manufacture and test, of any of the eight factories engaged in the venture on either side of the Channel. It was the largest single source airframe component supplier to both the British and French Concorde final assembly centres at Filton (Bristol) and Toulouse respectively. Complementing its Concorde workshare, an important new work pattern emerged at Weybridge during the 1970s, whereby the proud Vickers-Weybridge aircraft family gave way to a widely-varied work pattern during the final years. This involved an advanced multi-product, multi-national overall work programme, embracing major contributions to more than ten UK, European and North American civil and military aircraft, as well as smaller ones to several more: a programme in which the skill and the fame of the erstwhile Vickers-Weybridge team continued to operate in the forefront of the global aeronautical enterprise.

It could justifiably be claimed then that the Anglo-French Concorde and Jaguar; the Anglo-German-Italian Tornado; the European Airbus A300, A310 and A320 family; the British Aerospace Harrier, Hawk, 748, ATP, 146, 125, Jetstream and VC10 Tanker conversion (at Bristol); Shorts SD330; the Lockheed Tristar and the (Rolls-Royce powered) Boeing 747 programmes, all incorporated, in one area or another, the distinctive 'Designed and/or made or supported at Weybridge' label. The Weybridge team was also responsible for early developments of carbon-fibre structures and the world's first 'glass' cockpit (of which the Weybridge development facility is now exhibited at the National Air and Space Museum in the Smithsonian Institution at Washington DC, USA).

After seventeen years under the BAC banner, the original Vickers aviation team at Weybridge and Hurn bequeathed its exceptional heritage and experience to British Aerospace (BAe) on its 'vesting' on 29 April 1977 through nationalisation (when Vickers Limited lost both its aviation and shipbuilding assets at a stroke) and formal constitution on 1 January 1978. Thus mainstream involvement in aviation by Vickers came to an end just months short of seventy years since its pioneering beginning on 21 July 1908. Progressive rationalisation of the (later privatised) very large and geographically widespread BAe operation resulted in the closure first of the Hurn plant in 1984, followed by the parent factory at Weybridge in 1988.

The last operational vestige of the original Vickers-Weybridge site fronting Brooklands Road – the British Aerospace out-of-London headquarters – also disappeared in 1990 with its transfer to Farnborough. Occurring just seventy-five years after the emergence of the first Farnborough-designed and Vickers-built aircraft at Weybridge, the BE2c, in 1915, this event was both historic and futuristic. (A major commercial aircraft spares logistic centre continues to operate on the west side of the Brooklands site and is now under the aegis of the new European commercial aircraft company, Air International (Regional), of which British Aerospace is a prime partner.)

Legacy and Epitaph

The Vickers' aeronautical epoch spanned seventy crowded and eventful years during which many of the best standards were set that others were keen to follow. More than 17,000 aircraft, of more than sixty distinctly different basic types built by Vickers, continue to be symbolised by the VC10 and Super VC10, still in global service with the Royal Air Force – always Vickers biggest and most important customer – and in Vickers' major contribution to the Concorde (which has daily saluted Brooklands for more than twenty years), as well as through the important role which the Vickers-Weybridge team played in the establishment of European industrial collaboration that is now such a powerful force in world-wide commercial and military aviation and defence.

There are many good reasons, therefore, why Vickers PLC, British Aerospace and indeed the entire British and European aerospace enterprise should be proud to have benefited from the rich and creative heritage which the Vickers aviation endeavour has bequeathed to them. Although the historic Vickers-Weybridge aircraft factory closed (1988) and was demolished for redevelopment of the site, the traditional 'Vickers Spirit' has since been recreated in an imaginative renaissance at the Spirit of Brooklands Museum where many of the key Vickers aircraft types and the proud and accomplished Vickers' aviation record are represented and preserved for public appreciation and posterity.

From left to right: R.K. ('Rex') Pierson CBE. Renowned Vickers Chief Designer from 1917 to 1948, who joined Vickers at Erith in 1908 at the age of 17 and, during his highly distinguished forty year career, was responsible for thirty-six basic Vickers designs with more than 140 variants ranging from the Vickers Vimy (1917) to the conception of the Viscount in the late 1940s. He died in January 1948 aged only 56. Sir Robert McLean. Forceful Chairman of Vickers (Aviation) Ltd and of Vickers-Supermarine in the 1930s who persuaded the Air Ministry to accept the Vickers' design for the Wellesley monoplane long-range bomber instead of the mediocre biplane which they had specified. He fought similarly hard for Supermarine, rejecting the mediocre official fighter specification in favour of Reginald Mitchell's Spitfire. Major Sir Hew Kilner MC. After distinguished Army service in the First World War, Hew Kilner joined Vickers in 1930, was appointed General Manager of the Aircraft Section in 1940 and Managing Director (Aviation) in 1944. Knighted in 1947 for outstanding organisation and leadership of the Vickers-Armstrongs wartime production effort, he continued to head Vickers' aviation operations into the post-war jet age until his death at the age of only 61. Sir George Edwards OM CBE FRS FEng DL. He joined Vickers at Weybridge in 1935 aged 27 and over the next forty years became Britain's most outstanding aircraft designer and industrial leader, responsible for the distinctive Vickers' post-war aircraft and was the British mentor for the Anglo-French Concorde, the foundation of the modern pan-European aerospace industrial alliances. Succeeding Rex Pierson in 1948 and Sir Hew Kilner in 1953, he was awarded the CBE in 1952, knighted in 1957 and awarded the Order of Merit in 1971 before his retirement as Chairman of the British Aircraft Corporation in 1975.

One

Airships:
Britain's First to Last

When Vickers embarked on the design and construction of Britain's first Zeppelin-type airship, the HMA No.1 at its Barrow-in-Furness shipyard in 1908, the result suffered catastrophic structural failure on completion in 1911. The scalar similarity with shipbuilding was completely offset by the incompatibility of the respective structural concepts. However, the company was undeterred and two years later, under Hartley B. Pratt, assisted by a young Barnes Wallis, the first British airship to fly successfully, the HMA No.9, was produced. It was the mathematical ingenuity of Wallis, a former shipbuilding apprentice, who resolved this dichotomy and three more Vickers rigid- and three Parseval-type non-rigid airships followed, together with several SS (Sea Scout) Blimps, under the design leadership of Wallis before his trans-Atlantic R100 airship of 1929 was the last British airship in view of the horrendous loss of the government-sponsored R101 in October 1930.

Vickers was thus concerned with rigid airships for twenty-two years – longer than any manufacturer other than the German Zeppelin Company. Although it lost money over the whole period, it did have the distinction of having built the first British rigid airship, and the last.

The first British airship, the Vickers HMA (His Majesty's Airship) No.1, approbriously nicknamed 'Mayfly', undergoing initial mooring trials at the company's Cavendish Dock, Barrow. Despite considerable structural changes involving transposition of the fore and aft engines and propellers, it suffered an amidships break-up on 24 September 1911 when struck by a sudden gust of wind as it was being manoeuvred from it construction shed.

The Vickers HMA No.9 of 1916, the company's second rigid airship, under the design direction of Barnes Wallis at a new airship works at nearby Walney Island, for the training of crews for later airships. This was the first British airship to fly successfully. Of duralumin construction with steel strengthening, it incorporated multiple horizontal control surfaces for ease of manoeuvring. Of 540 ft in length and with a capacity of 880,000 cu ft, it had a designed gross lift of 26.5 tons. It was powered by four 180 hp Wolesley-Maybach engines, the front two of which were also equipped with Vickers patented swivelling gear.

The Vickers HMA No.23, the third Vickers airship, of 1915. An enlarged version of the company's second, the HMA No.9, it was the first of the 23 class, which included No.24 by Beardmore and No.25 by Armstrong Whitworth, both to the Vickers design, because this was the number in the consecutive order of Royal Navy airships, including the Farnborough Army airships which had been taken over for naval use. The Vickers No.26 was the first to bear the prefix 'R' to signify Rigid. The Vickers 23 and R.26 airships were delivered in October 1917 and March 1918 respectively and were used for patrols over the North Sea and for training. The Vickers R.80 airship which followed in 1924 was the ultimate in the Wallis development of the streamline shape.

One of the several SS (Sea Scout) Blimps built by the Vickers Airship Department. These small non-rigid airships were mainly used for searching narrow sea channels, such as the Dover Straights and the Irish narrows, from their bases at Capel (Folkstone) and Polegate (Eastbourne), and also in the Mediterranean.

A typical Vickers-built Blimp at an East Coast Royal Naval Air Station in 1915 with its adapted early BE2c fuselage serving as a control car. Vickers also built three Parseval-type non-rigid airships (a successful contemporary German design) – P.5, P.6, and P.7 – at Barrow, under licence from the German Luft-Fahrzeug Gesellschaft, the owners of the Parseval patents, in a programme approved by Winston Churchill, then First Lord of the Admiralty, and of which the flight trials were completed in December 1917. Like the Blimps, they were used primarily for patrol duties off the East Coast over the North Sea.

A Vickers Blimp together with a Vickers Type 54 Viking Mk.IV amphibian F-ADBL built for the French Section Technique in 1921. These non-rigid Sea Scout airships had a capacity of 70,000 cu ft and a length of 144 ft and were operated by a crew of two sitting in the BE-type aeroplane fuselage suspended from the airship envelope by wire ropes. They had a 1,000-mile range at 35 mph, and, powered by an 80 hp Renault or similar engine, had a top speed of 45 mph. They carried out many patrols along the East Coast.

The 709 ft long Vickers R.100 airship under construction in its shed at the disused Royal Naval Air Station at Howden, Yorkshire, which had been purchased by the Airship Guarantee Company for £61,000. Design was begun by Barnes Wallis at Vickers House in London in 1924, continued at the company's engineering works at Crayford, Kent, and finally transferred alongside the construction at Howden.

The Vickers R.100 airship at the fabric-covering stage of assembly for gas-bag retention at Howden.

The Vickers long-distance airship R.100 G-FAAV on its mooring mast at Howden. It was first flown on 16 December 1929, arrived at Cardington, Bedfordshire, 2 hours later and went on to make an endurance flight of 54 hours, mostly in fog, over Southern England and the Channel. A specification-proving trans-Atlantic flight to Canada and back was completed in July and August 1930, the outward flight time being 78 hours at an average speed of 42 mph against the prevailing headwinds, and homeward bound 58 hours. However, the final cost of the R.100 was about £570,000, some £220,000 in excess of the contract price. It was sold for scrap in 1931 and the Airship Guarantee Company finally went into liquidation on 30 November 1935.

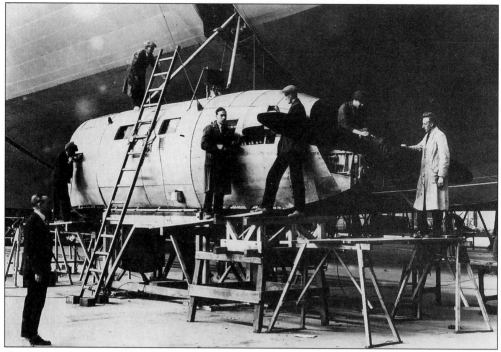

Construction of one of the control cars of the Vickers R.100 airship.

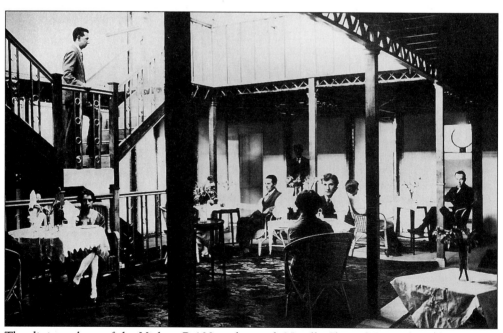

The dining saloon of the Vickers R.100 airship with Neville Shute (Norway) on the stairs to the promenade deck. Shute was the assistant designer of the R.100 working with Barnes Wallis and took part in its trans-Atlantic flight, dramatically telling its story in his well-known book *Slide Rule*.

Two
Early Monoplanes and Fighting Biplanes

Undeterred by the failure of its first airship in 1911, that same year Vickers elected to enter the fledgling aircraft business by establishing an aviation department in part of its engineering works at Erith, Kent, with a drawing office at Vickers House, Broadway, Westminster. With no prior technical knowledge, the company prudently secured a licence for a French design from Robert Esnault Pelterie (REP) of Paris and from which stemmed a series of eight braced monoplanes which were mainly used by Vickers at the flying school which it set up in 1912 at Brooklands, near Weybridge in Surrey, the scene of much of the early British pioneering effort in aviation. Boxkite-type pusher biplanes prompted the advantages of this layout for carrying a nose-mounted machine-gun. The result was the famous Vickers Gunbus genus of fighting biplanes, which were also built in France and gave excellent service during the First World War.

Allocated substantial contracts for designs emanating from the government-owned Royal Aircaft Factory at Farnborough, during the First World War Vickers built nearly 3,000 aircraft at its Kent factories at Erith, Crayford and Bexleyheath and at Brooklands, where its aviation facilities were then progressively concentrated from 1915.

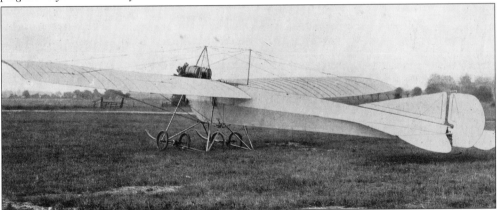

Vickers first aeroplane, the two-seat No.1 Monoplane, at Brooklands. Built at the Erith works of Vickers, Sons and Maxim, and first flown at Joyce Green, near Dartford, Kent, in July 1911, it had a fan-type REP engine and part REP airframe (rear fuselage), and was otherwise made by Vickers of REP-type steel-tube construction. It also incorporated a form of pilot control embodying a single control column which in broad principle remains today (but which subsequently cost Vickers £40,000 in litigation for alleged infringement of REP patents). This historic Vickers aircraft was sold to Dr (later Sir) Douglas Mawson for the 1912 Australian Antarctic Expedition, but crashed on a trial flight in October 1911 in Adelaide. Its remains were used as an air-tractor sledge, parts of which are preserved in Australia, and others have been sighted in Mawson's hut at Cape Denison, the base for the expedition only recently.

Staff of the Vickers Flying School at Brooklands posing in front of the Vickers-REP monoplane. Under the propeller boss is Robert Barnwell, chief instructor and, also with cap, Archie Knight, assistant instructor, who later became the Vickers Works Manager at Weybridge.

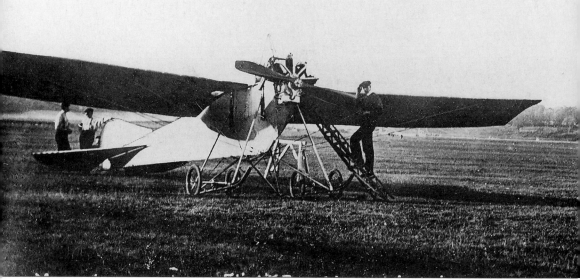

The Vickers No.2. Monoplane at Brooklands, completed in September 1911 which, with the next three, was also used by the Vickers Flying School. It had an elaborate two-skid, four-wheel, well-sprung undercarriage and a giraffe-type pilot's steps.

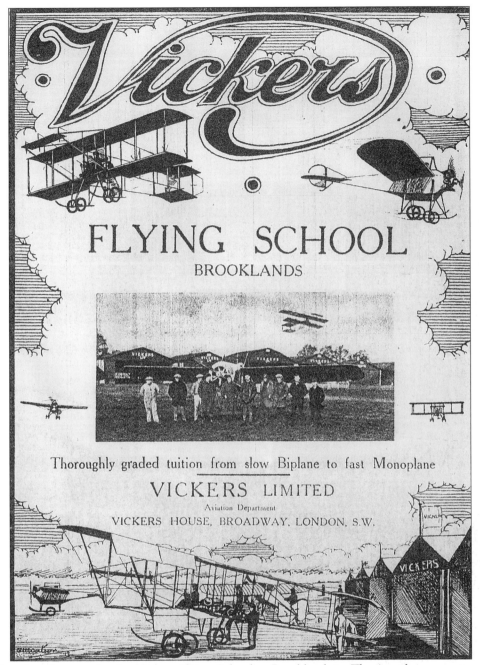

An advertisement for the Vickers Flying School at Brooklands in *The Aeroplane* magazine of 13 November 1913. Established in sheds Nos 37, 38, 39 and 40 near the Byfleet banking, between 1912 and the outbreak of the First World War in August 1914 (when it was taken over by the Royal Flying Corps), the Vickers School trained seventy-seven pupils including such distinguished names as Sir Sefton Branker, the first Director of Civil Aviation (who lost his life in the R.101 airship distaster of 1930); Marshal of the Royal Air Force Viscount Trenchard, 'Father of the Royal Air Force'; Air Chief Marshal Lord Dowding, the director of the Battle of Britain and Rex Pierson, the renowned Vickers Chief Designer.

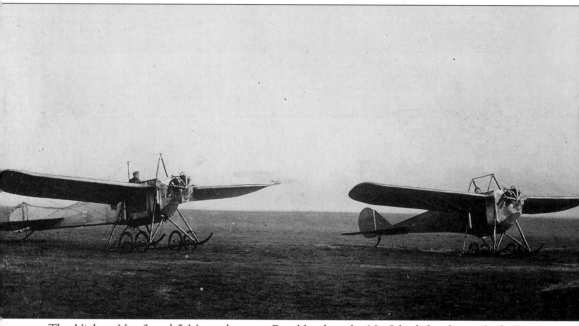

The Vickers Nos 3 and 5 Monoplanes at Brooklands – the No.5 had the deeper body; No.4 closely resembled No.5.

The side-by-side, two-seat, Vickers No.6 Monoplane built at Erith in 1912, unofficially known as the Vickers *Sociable*. Fitted with a 670 hp Viale seven-cylinder engine radial engine and a Levasseur-type propeller, it was a considerable advance on its predecessors. Re-engined with the more reliable 80 hp Gnome rotary engine, it was entered in the War Office Military Aeroplane Trials at Larkhill, Salisbury Plain, in 1912 and flown by Vickers' pilot L.F. Macdonald. A biplane conversion of this aircraft was also flown by Macdonald but he and his mechanic were both drowned when it crashed into the Thames on 13 January 1913.

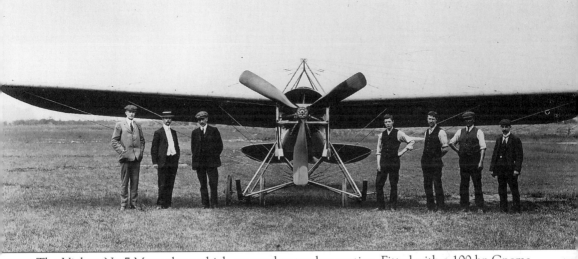

The Vickers No.7 Monoplane which reverted to tandem seating. Fitted with a 100 hp Gnome rotary engine and a three-bladed propeller, it had the undercarriage arrangement of the Nos 1 to 5 Monoplanes.

The Vickers No.8 Monoplane with side-by-side seating (as on the No.6), the last in the series built at Erith, packed for field transport to Brooklands on a trailer towed by a Napier car complete with ground crew. The British War Office had lost confidence in monoplanes following some accidents in 1912. For five months from September 1912, military pilots were not permitted to fly monoplanes in the Royal Flying Corps and this was the turning point after which Vickers used the biplane layout.

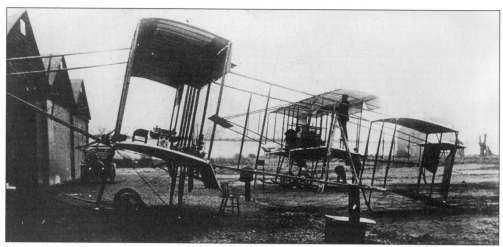

One of three Farman-type, unequal-span, pusher biplanes purchased from Vickers next-door neighbour at Brooklands, Hewlett and Blondeau, towards the end of 1912 and which, with some reconstruction, became known as the Vickers *Boxkite* (with a Howard Wright biplane in the background). An equal-span version appeared in December 1913 with a primitive enclosed seating nacelle for instructor and pupil which became known as the Vickers *Pumpkin*. A somewhat similar design was the Vickers *Hydravion*, intended for operation from land or water and for which duralumin floats were made at the Vickers Dartford works and tested for corrosion in the nearby River Darent.

The Vickers Experimental Fighting Biplane EFB.1 on display at the 1913 Aero Show at Olympia and named *Destroyer*. Although the Vickers-Challenger interruptor-gear had been invented to enable a fixed gun to fire through a revolving tractor propeller, progressive design development of the *Boxkite/Hydravion* pusher concept led Vickers to see this as the best solution for an offensive military aeroplane. The linking of the company's interests in armaments and aviation then received practical recognition from the Admiralty on 19 November 1912 with a request for an experimental fighting biplane armed with a machine-gun. Although Vickers did build a tractor scout biplane, the S.B.1, in 1914, this was abandoned in favour of the EFB.1 which marked the beginning of Vickers' military aircraft lineage with its successful Gunbus family.

28

One of the the four Vickers F.B.5As built at Bexleyheath with an armour-plated nose and vee-type undercarriage, typifying the Vickers F.B.5/9 Gunbus genus which evolved through a series of experimental predecessors. Of the first three 100 hp Gnome-powered F.B.5s built at the Vickers Crayford factory (which took over production) delivered to No.6 Squadron of the Royal Flying Corps at Netheravon in November 1914, two were returned to the company's airfield at Joyce Green, Dartford, to create the nucleus of the air defence of London.

A Vickers F.B.9 Gunbus on the Western Front in winter snow at Christmas 1915. Some were also used in the Battle of the Somme in 1916. A total of 214 F.B.5/9 Gunbus aircraft were built by Vickers (160 at Crayford, 4 at Bexleyheath and 50 at Weybridge). The French company, S.A. Darracq of Suresnes, also made 99 F.B.5s and F.B.9s under licence. Six were built in Denmark as single-seaters for the Danish Army. In 1915, Snd Lt G.S.M. Insall was awarded the Victoria Cross for gallantry after forcing down a German Aviatik reconnaissance machine while flying a Vickers Gunbus.

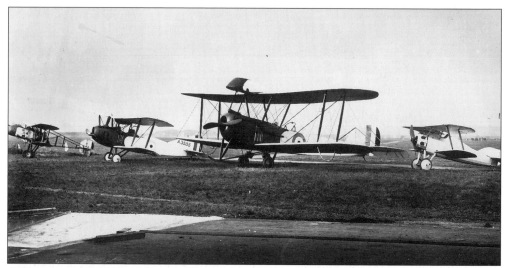

A line-up of Vickers' experimental aircraft at Joyce Green, Dartford, airfield. Left to right: F.B.12C, F.B.14, F.B.11 and F.B.16.

Large-scale production at Weybridge of the famous wartime S.E.5a biplane fighter that was designed by H.P. Folland at the Royal Aircraft Factory, Farnborough. Vickers built 1,650 S.E.5as at Weybridge, by far the highest share of the total national output of 5,205 aircraft built between 1917 and 1919. Vickers also built 515 S.E.5as at Crayford and 431 were also made by the Vickers' subsidiary, Wolseley Motors. A splendid non-flying replica of a Weybridge-made S.E.5a is currently being built at the Brooklands Museum to represent this impressive early Vickers' quantity-production achievement.

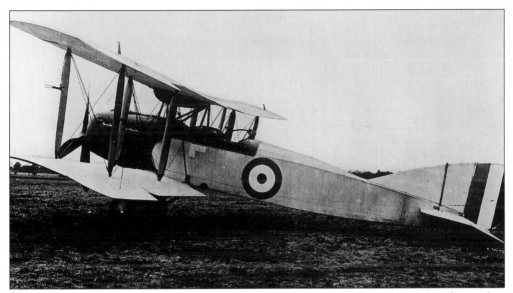

The Vickers F.B.14D general-purpose single-engined tractor biplane of 1916 with two-bay wings and powered by a Rolls-Royce Eagle engine. The Vickers F.B.14 was intended as a replacement for the Farnborough-designed B.E.2 series in Middle East squadrons. Several were sent to Mesopotamia and seven were used by Home Defence squadrons. It was also from the F.B.14 that the Vickers' lineage of tractor biplanes of the inter-war years descended. In the F.B.14D (Sir) Vernon Brown (pilot) and (Sir) Melville Jones (observer) shot down a Gotha bomber off Zeebrugge on the Belgian coast in July 1917 with an ingenious gunsight invented by Jones which made allowance for the relative speeds of opposing aircraft and for wind velocity.

The Vickers E.S.1 was adapted from the private-venture 'Barnwell Bullet' small high-speed Scout designed by Harold Barnwell, who had been appointed Chief Test Pilot by Vickers after the closure of their flying school at Brooklands. It came to grief on its first flight by its designer so its redesign into the Vickers Experimental Scout E.S.1 was entrusted to Rex Pierson, a young graduate apprentice then in the drawing office. Also adapted into the E.S.2, it was flown before King George V during his visit to Crayford in September 1915.

One of twelve Vickers F.B.19 Mk.II (the second derivative of a development of the Barnwell Bullet) shipped to Archangel for the Imperial Russian Air Service in 1917 but which remained in their crates when the revolution of that year intervened; they are believed to have been destroyed by British Forces in 1919. About 50 F.B.19 Mk.Is and the 12 Mk.IIs were made at Weybridge and were used in small numbers on the Western Front, in Macedonia and Palestine.

The Vickers F.B.26A Vampire II with a 230 hp Bentley B.R.2 pusher rotary engine and twin nose-mounted machine guns. It was originally intended as a single-seat night fighter but the contract went to the Sopwith Salamander. It was during an evening test flight on 25 August 1917 that Harold Barnwell was killed in one of these aircraft at Joyce Green, Dartford. The F.B.26A was the culmination of Vickers long and varied series of both tractor and pusher biplane fighter designs and the last of the single-seat pusher fighters of the First World War.

Three

The Pioneering Vimy and the Bomber-Transports

The emergence of the brilliant Rex Pierson as Vickers Chief Designer in 1917 at the age of only twenty-six was to result in one of the most accomplished and famous aircraft of all time – the Vickers Vimy biplane bomber. Although the Armistice in November 1918 precluded active service during the First World War, the Vimy not only pioneered some of the world's great airlanes of today but also led to an impressive range of bomber-transports which formed the backbone of this capability in the Royal Air Force during much of the inter-war period.

The outstanding significance of the Vickers bomber-transport family was stated by Air Marshal Sir Denis Barnett, AOC-in-C RAF Transport Command, in his address to the Institute of Transport in 1960, when he said, 'Between the two wars, the thinking generated by the First found its expression, until the Second drew near, in the development of that celebrated family of maids-of-all-work, the family of (Vickers) bomber-transport aircraft which had their culmination in the Valentia. Any story told during those years would be embellished brightly by the rich diversity and enduring value of those squadrons. Indeed, our modern networks of worldwide routes owe much more than is customarily remembered today to their imaginative and pioneering exertions'.

Shortly after the start of the First World War, Vickers engaged Howard Flanders to design a new twin-engined fighting aeroplane to carry a Vickers' one-pounder gun. Classified as the E.F.B.7 when it first flew in August 1915, it vied with the French Caudron for the claim of being the first twin-engined military aircraft to fly successfully. However, it was the Rex Pierson development seen here, the E.F.B.8 of November 1915, which proved to be the inspiration of his design of a new twin-engined bomber requested from Vickers by the Air Board in 1917, when Pierson was made Chief Designer, which became the famous Vickers Vimy.

The prototype Vickers F.B.27 Vimy in final assembly at Joyce Green in 1917. For its roll-out the floor had to be recessed to provide adequate height clearance for the completed machine. The four F.B.27 prototypes were fitted with 200 hp geared Hispano Suizas (later re-engined with 260 hp Salmsons, 200 hp Sunbeam Maoris, 300 hp Fiat A-12s, and 360 hp Rolls-Royce Eagle VIIIs respectively). The official name Vimy (after the famous wartime battleground) was introduced in 1918.

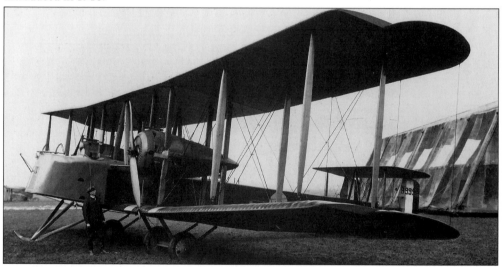

The first Vickers Vimy prototype B9952 (later G-EAAR) when re-engined with Salmson water-cooled radial engines. The original designing, building and flying of this machine (by Gordon Bell at Joyce Green on 30 November 1917) was completed in only four months and the fourth prototype, powered by Rolls-Royce Eagles, went to the newly-formed Aeroplane Experimental Establishment at Martlesham Heath in Suffolk on 11 October 1918. However, intended as a long-range heavy bomber to attack targets deep inside Germany, including Berlin, the Armistice in November 1918 intervened and the Vimy was not used operationally in the First World War.

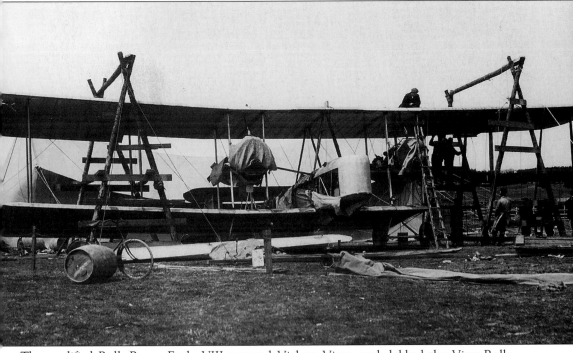

The modified Rolls-Royce Eagle VIII-powered Vickers Vimy, and dubbed the Vimy-Rolls, being erected at Quidi Vidi airfield, near St Johns, in Newfoundland, before being flown to Lester's Field for take-off to become the world's first aeroplane to make a trans-Atlantic flight non-stop, in the hands of Capt John Alcock and Lt Arthur Whitten Brown, on 14/15 June 1919.

The moment of take-off by the Vickers Vimy-Rolls from Newfoundland on 14 June 1919 – a defining moment in the history of both British and world aviation.

The somewhat undignified end of the first-ever direct Atlantic aerial crossing by the Vickers Vimy-Rolls – in the Derrygimla bog at Clifden, County Galway, Southern Ireland, on 15 June 1919 – after the 16 hr 27 min 1,890-mile flight though appalling weather conditions which included the night of 14 June. Fully restored, this historic Vickers aircraft is today on public display in the Aeronautical Gallery of the Science Museum, London. A most impressive flying replica, which (like that of the Vickers Gunbus of 1966) was built by the Vintage Aircraft and Flying Association at Weybridge in 1969 to celebrate the 50th anniversary of this epic flight, is now displayed at the RAF Museum at Hendon.

Widely and deservedly feted, and winning the £10,000 prize sponsored by the London *Daily Mail*, both Alcock and Brown were knighted for their heroic and pioneering achievement – made only sixteen years after the dawn of powered flight itself.

The Vickers Vimy G-EAOU (euphemistically translated as 'God 'Elp All Of Us') at the point of take-off for Australia on 12 November 1919 from the old Hounslow airfield, about two miles east of the present London Heathrow Airport. This second great Vimy intercontinental flight was made in pursuit of the £10,000 prize offered by the Australian Government. The arduous 11,250-mile journey to Darwin was completed in just under 28 days on 10 December 1919. G-EAOU is today preserved at Adelaide, home of the pilots, in a building for which the Australian public subscribed £A30,000. The 75th anniversary of this epic flight was recreated in 1994 with a superb replica courageously flown by its mentors, American Peter McMillan and Australian Lang Kidby (and now back in the UK).

The brothers Capt Ross Smith (left) and Lt Keith Smith (right) who made the first England-to-Australia flight in the Vickers Vimy G-EAOU, with Sgts W.H. Shiers and J.M. Bennett as their engineers. Like Alcock and Brown, the Smith brothers were both later knighted.

The standard military-type Vickers Vimy G-UABA *Silver Queen* on the compass base at Brooklands being inspected by Lt Col Pierre Van Ryneveld and Major C. J. Quintin Brand of the South African Air Force before their attempt to fly from England to Cape Town. Leaving Brooklands on 4 February 1920, they crashed at Korosko, between Cairo and Khartoum, a week later due to a leaking radiator. A second Vimy named *Silver Queen* II, loaned by the RAF in Egypt, reached Bulawayo in Southern Rhodesia where it failed to lift off again due to dirty engine oil. Undeterred, the crew borrowed a de Havilland D.H.9 and completed the flight to be awarded £5,000 by the South African Government. They too were knighted by King George V.

The prototype Vimy Commercial K-107 (later G-EAAV) which took off from Brooklands on 24 January 1920 for another attempt to fly to South Africa. Chartered from Vickers by *The Times*, with Dr Chalmers Mitchell as their Press representative, it crashed at Tabora, Tanganyika, on 27 February, failing to take-off in tropical conditions due to contaminated water in the engine cooling system. Nevertheless, the lessons learnt from these pioneering African Vimy flights were fully applied later to the successful use of the Vimy and its military successors in Egypt, the Middle East and India.

The morning departure of the Vickers Vimy Commercial from Heliopolis, Cairo, on 6 February 1920 by Vickers pilots, Stan Cockerell and Tommy Broome, during the third African Vimy flight.

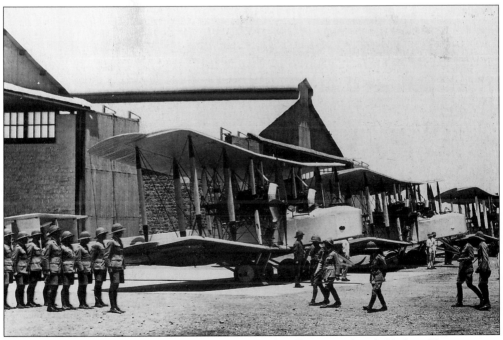

AOC's inspection of No.4 FTS (Flight Training School) equipped with Vickers Vimy trainers at Abu Sueir, Egypt, in 1930.

Bristol Jupiter-engined Vickers Vimy trainers of the Royal Air Force Parachute Training School at Henlow, Bedfordshire. A night-flying unit equipped with Vimys operated from Biggin Hill, Kent, long after the type had disappeared from the rest of the RAF. The Vimy also continued to be used up to the time of the Munich crisis in 1938 as a target aircraft for the searchlight crews of the Royal Engineers training at Blackdown, Hampshire. The Vimy H651 was also used at the RAE Farnborough in 1923 for original experiments with automatic landing.

The ten-passenger Vickers F.B.28 Vimy Commercial G-EASI, named *City of London*, taking-off from Croydon for Paris (the air route which it opened up in 1920) in its first livery of the shipping line and pioneering airline, S. Instone and Co., before wearing that of Imperial Airways with which Instone was later merged. Both of these airlines were original predecessors of British Airways. G-EASI was in service for five years on various European short-haul routes and was thus dubbed 'The Father of the Airliner'. By 1 April 1924, this aircraft had flown 108,000 miles and carried many thousands of passengers.

The first of five military ambulance versions of the Vickers Vimy Commercial of 1921, J6855 was produced for the RAF to carry four stretcher or eight sitting cases, with two medical staff in attendance, the stretchers being loaded through a door in the nose – probably the first instance of nose-loading. Powered by two 450 hp Napier Lion II engines, five of these Vimy Ambulance versions were built. They were later converted to Vernon standard and used by Nos 45 and 70 Squadrons.

A Russian photograph of the so-called Vimy Commercial supplied to Russia in 1922 reveals its true identity as a hybrid Vickers Vernon with Napier Lion engines. Although there is no surviving information about its use, it is believed to have been flown in the Moscow area. A Vickers' service engineer, who went to Russia with this aircraft and a Vickers Viking IV amphibian, was given the impression that the acquisition of such aircraft by the Russians was to familiarise themselves with the latest Western ideas and practices.

A line-up of Rolls-Royce Eagle VIII powered Vickers Vernon I military transports of the Royal Air Force in the Middle East. The Vernon was the RAF's first transport aircraft.

A Vickers Vernon Mk.III rebuilt from a Vimy Ambulance, hence its serial number JR6904 – 'R' meaning reconditioned. The standard nosewheel was also deleted from this Mark. Following directly from the Vimy Commercial and the Vimy Ambulance, the Vernon was originally called a Troop Transport, but later classified as a Bomber-Transport, like the subsequent Victoria and Valentia; also it was in these military service roles that it was widely used. The Vernon was also the first RAF aircraft to be specifically operated as the transport equipment of an emergency fire brigade, to quell violence in Cyprus and among the tribes of the mandated territory of Iraq. The Vernon II also operated the Cairo-Baghdad air mail service in the early 1920s.

The first Vickers Vulcan six-to-eight passenger commercial transport, G-EBBL, in early 1922 in the livery of Instone Air Line Ltd. Powered by a single 360 hp Rolls-Royce Eagle VIII engine, a triangular fin was later fitted centrally above the upper tailplane to improve the yaw characteristics of the type. Although not strictly in the Vimy lineage, the design of the Vulcan borrowed heavily from the capacious fuselage design of the transport derivatives of the Vimy but for which the Vulcan was nicknamed 'The Flying Pig'. A 450 hp Napier Lion-powered version was also operated by Imperial Airways.

Parachute training with the Vickers Virginia X military bomber by means of the 'pull-off' method at the Home Aircraft Depot, Henlow, on Empire Air Day in 1935. By this method, the pupil stood on a platform fixed to the wing and at a given signal, pulled the rip-cord. The opening of the parachute carried him from the aircraft so that he was actually airborne when he left it. The family resemblance between the Virginia and the original Vimy is clearly evident. The first Virginia was delivered to the RAF in December 1932. A total of 126 were built in several versions and served widely with seven RAF Squadrons until late 1937. The Virginia also won the Lawrence Minot Trophy five times for its bombing prowess.

A dramatic forward view from the tail gunner's position of the Vickers Virginia Mk.X J7130 fitted experimentally with Bristol Pegasus engines, Townend exhaust collector rings, and used as an armament test aircraft.

Pioneering in-flight refuelling experiments with the Vickers Virginia Mk.X J7275 acting as the tanker and passing fuel though a flexible hose to a Westland Wapiti receiver aircraft. These tests were made with several different types of receiver aircraft during many flights from Farnborough and Ford (Hampshire) aerodromes and the system was demonstrated at the 1936 Hendon Air Display.

A formation of Vickers Victoria III military transports flying over the familiar landmark of the Egyptian Pyramids. Among the many duties performed by the Victoria were blind flying training and 'sky-shouting' to marauding tribes during air police duties in the Middle East when four loud-speakers were fitted to Victoria V K2345. Eight Vickers Victorias (and one HP Hinaidi) transports of No. 70 Squadron RAF conducted the world's first major airlift by evacuating 586 civilians from the British Legation in Kabul, Afganistan, between 23 December 1928 and 25 February 1929 following the Shiamwari tribal uprising. Ninty-seven Victorias were built which served with six RAF Squadrons, more than half of which were also converted to the Valentia by fitting 650 hp Bristol Pegasus IIM series engines.

The Vickers Valentia military transport K3602 with a capacity for twenty-two fully-armed troops, one of the first sixteen aircraft delivered to the RAF between May and November 1934. After several names had been suggested for this last variant of the original Vimy lineage, although Valentia had been applied to an earlier Vickers flying-boat, it was never used by any of the Services and so it was finally agreed for the transport type in February 1934. Twenty-eight Valentias were built and fifty-four conversions made from the Victoria, many of them by the RAF in the Middle East.

Built to a design initiated in 1921 for a 23-seat commercial transport, with later interest from the Air Ministry to Specification 1/22, the resulting Vickers Vanguard biplane was given both the military serial J6924 and the civil registration G-EBCP when delivered to Imperial Airways in May 1928 for operation from Croydon on loan from the Air Ministry. Although it performed well, regrettably this single example was the only civil derivative of the Victoria/Valentia concept which played such a great part in the development of military transport between the wars. Nevertheless, it did achieve a world load-carrying record on 6 July 1928. Unfortunately, G-EBCP crashed at Shepperton while being test flown with a modified tail unit, killing Tiny Scholefield, Vickers Chief Test Pilot.

The Vickers Type 150 B.19/27 experimental bomber in its original form in November 1929, with two 480 hp Rolls-Royce FXIVS engines and retractable radiators under the top centre section. Based on the Vickers Virginia, for which it was conceived as a replacement, during the extensive evaluation (including in-flight refuelling with a Boulton Paul Overstrand) it was developed through the Type 163 to the Type 195/255 Vanox when re-engined with two 600 hp Bristol Pegasus IM3 engines. However, a cooling of Air Ministry interest meant that quantity production did not occur. A second Vickers B.19/27 was the private-venture Type 163 powered by four 480 hp Rolls-Royce FXIVS (Kestrel) engines installed in a push-pull layout.

Four

The Inter-War
Intermediaries

Alongside the development of the Vimy biplane bomber-transport genus, like most other contemporary British aircraft manufacturing companies, Vickers tendered for numerous other inter-war commercial and military opportunities with varying degrees of success. Immediately after the First World War, the Viking amphibian not only achieved significant exports but also provided the starting product for the Canadian Vickers air arm established in 1922. From the Vixen military tractor biplane of the early 1920s stemmed a series of variants culminating in the Vildebeest and Vincent torpedo-carriers, both of which saw service in the early part of the Second World War.

The Wibault patented structural design system of the 1920s was a useful step in the development of all-metal airframes and the monoplane layout, being realised in both military and commercial types. The production of large batches of Armstrong Whitworth Siskins and Hawker Harts also helped to keep the Vickers-Weybridge factory busy during some of the lean years. After a wide range of biplane and monoplane fighters, it was Reginald Mitchell's brilliant Spitfire, produced by the Vickers-Supermarine partner company, which was to fulfil this primary requirement so magnificently – while the Vickers-Weybridge team concentrated on its geodetic bomber lineage.

The prototype Vickers Viking amphibian G-EAOV, Vickers first venture into flying boats, was built in two months and first flown at Brooklands in November 1919. It was designed by Rex Pierson with a 270 hp Rolls-Royce Falcon III engine mounted pusher-fashion for unobstructed crew and passenger accommodation. Although Vickers had not previously handled this class of aeroplane, it did have the experience of S.E. Saunders and Co. of Cowes, Isle of Wight, then a Vickers' subsidiary, to rely on for the construction of the Linton Hope-type hull. Sadly, it was in this aircraft on 18 December 1919 that Sir John Alcock of trans-Atlantic Vimy fame only a few weeks earlier, and then Vickers Chief Test Pilot, was killed at Rouen when attempting a forced landing in fog enroute to the Paris Aero Show.

The Vickers Viking III, fitted with the more powerful 450 hp Napier Lion engine, taxying at Felixstowe during the Air Ministry Competitions in October 1920. Registered G-EAUK, it won the competition for amphibians and the first prize of £10,000.

The Vickers Viking III G-EAUK on the bank of the River Thames during its London-Paris centre-to-centre flights to the River Seine in 1921 by Stan Cockerell (who had replaced Sir John Alcock as Vickers Chief Test Pilot) in only two-and-a-half hours journey time – which compares favourably with both surface and aerial journey times between the two capitals today. This craft also won the 1920 Air Ministry contest for amphibians and the first prize of £10,000.

The Vickers Viking IV amphibian G-EBED, the second of two aircraft built for the planned round-the-world flight by Sir Ross Smith. Unfortunately, the first of the two, G-EBBZ, crashed on 13 April 1922 at Brooklands killing Sir Ross and Sgt Bennett (who had flown together on the historic first England-to-Australia flight by Vickers Vimy in November 1919). G-EBED was then sold to Capt Leslie Hamilton and used for a winter sports charter service between Croydon and St Moritz and Nice until it was scrapped in 1929. A non-flying replica of this aircraft is today exhibited at Brooklands Museum.

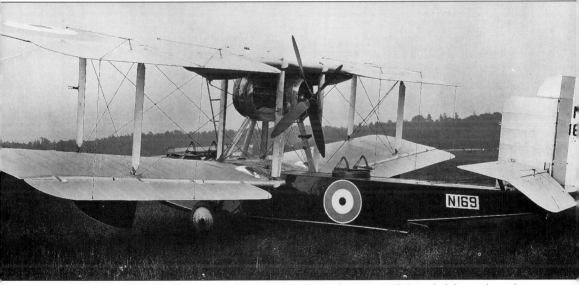

The Vickers Vanellus N169 built to Air Ministry Specification 46/22 and delivered to the Royal Aircraft Establishment at Farnborough on 25 August 1925 for comparative trials with the Supermarine Seagull III on HMS *Argus*. This was the second of the last two variants of the Vickers Viking amphibian – the Mk.VI Vulture and the Mk.VII Vanellus respectively. Total production of the Viking genus was 34 aircraft: 31 Viking (23 of which were exported to France, Holland, the Dutch East Indies, Japan, USA, Canada, Russia and Argentina); 2 Vulture and 1 Vanellus. The two Vultures were used for Sqn Ldr MacLaren's round-the-world attempt which started from Calshot on 25 March 1924 but which was abandoned in the Bering Sea near Nikolski off the Siberian coast because of the exceptional weather conditions encountered.

One the batch of 35 Vickers VIM (Vickers Instructional Machine) ordered by the Chinese Government in 1919, together with 40 Vimy Commercials and 20 reconditioned Avro 504Ks. The aim was to establish a civil aviation complex in China, but the results fell far short of expectations, probably because of Chinese political instability and cultural misunderstandings. The VIM was a rebuilt Farnborough-designed F.E.2d with a Rolls-Royce Eagle VIII pusher engine and redesigned dual-control crew nacelle.

The Vickers Viget Type 89 G-EBHN single-seat entry designed by Rex Pierson for the 1923 Lympne (Kent) Light Aeroplane Competitions for motor-gliders ie. light aeroplanes with low-powered engines. It was fitted with a 750 cc Douglas flat-twin engine and flown by Stan Cockerell, Vickers Chief Test Pilot.

The Vickers Vagabond Type 98 G-EBJF two-seat entry for the 1924 Light Aeroplane Competitions at Lympne, which were intended to foster private flying. Fitted with a 32 hp Bristol Cherub engine, it was flown by H.J. Payn, technical assistant to the designer, Rex Pierson. Payn had been technical assistant to Reginald Mitchell at Supermarine during the design of the Spitfire and now acted, from time-to-time, as a Vickers test pilot. The Vagabond also incorporated folding wings, with which feature Stan Cockerell had received public notoriety with the Vickers Viget the previous year after a forced landing. Stopping at a pub while pushing the aircraft home they were mistaken for a Punch and Judy show!

The 112 ft span Valentia flying-boat with a Vickers superstructure and Saunders Consuta-type (copper-wire sown) hull and powered by two 650 hp Rolls-Royce Condors, moored at Cowes, Isle of Wight, during flying and seaworthiness trials on the Solent in 1921. Vickers had bought a controlling interest in S.E. Saunders and Co. in 1918, but sold out in 1921. That company eventually became Saunders-Roe Ltd. The Air Ministry had placed a contract with Vickers for three flying-boats in May 1918, to be built at Barrow, based on the successful Porte-Felixstowe F.5 configuration, which they were intended to replace. In the event, the design and construction of this single prototype was completed by Saunders.

The Vickers Vixen II G-EBEC flown in August 1923, with longer fuselage, a faired-off nose and cleaner lines than the Vixen I. In 1922, Vickers had decided to design, as a private venture, a two-seat military tractor biplane fighter-reconaissance-bomber aircraft as a replacement for the Bristol Fighter or the D.H.9A. Based on its wartime F.B.14, but fitted with the more suitable 450 hp Napier Lion engine now available, it was sent to Martlesham for trials.

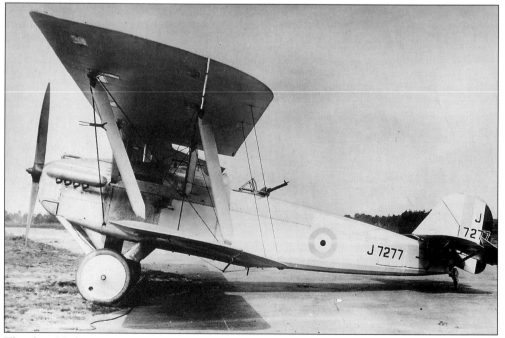

The first Vickers Venture J7277, which combined the Vixen II mainplanes, controls and propeller, the Vixen I fuel system and rigging, with the Vixen III extended fuselage, underslung radiator, tail and chassis, but of which only six were built. Chile bought eighteen Vixen Vs.

The Vickers Valparaiso I Type 93, fitted with a 468 hp Napier Lion IA engine, in Portuguese service (where it was also built under licence) and showing a combination of Vixen I and II features. The Rolls-Royce Eagle powered version was the Valparaiso II. The prototype Mk.I was sold to Chile and at the end of 1924 reached 20,000 ft, beating the existing height record of South America.

The Napier Lion-powered Vickers Vivid Type 130 G-EBPY two-seat general-purpose military biplane which resulted from a private venture reconstruction of the Vixen III, with an all-metal airframe. The name was suggested by Vickers test pilot, Capt Broome, then in Chile supervising the assembly and flying of Vixen Vs for the Chilean Air Force, who advised that an all-metal Vixen might be acceptable there. This aircraft was flown both as a landplane and a floatplane before being sold to J.R Chaplin in 1931 who, with Capt Neville Stack as pilot, set up out-and-back records from England to Berlin, Copenhagen and Warsaw.

The floatplane conversion of the Vickers Vivid being beached at the Avro seaplane base at Hamble. With Shorts-designed floats on a Vickers oleo-pneumatic chassis, it was flown to Felixstowe in May 1928 for a competition for a naval floatplane. In September 1928, after reverting to a landplane, Vickers test pilot Tiny Scholefield flew the aircraft to Bucharest, Romania, to participate in a competition for a general-purpose aeroplane for the Romanian Air Service, but no orders materialised.

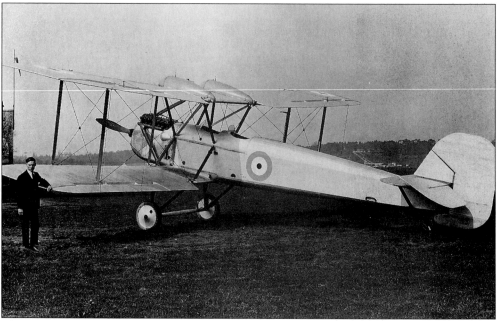

The Vickers Vendace I Type 120 N208 before delivery from Brooklands to Martlesham for military trials in 1926. Built in response to specification 5A/24 for a float seaplane for training purposes, it was powered by a 275 hp Rolls-Royce Falcon III engine and it was claimed that it could be converted from floats to wheels, or vice-versa, in only ten minutes.

The sole Vickers Vendace II G-EBPX which was a private venture demonstration landplane and seaplane and later, fitted with an ABC Nimbus engine, was sold in June 1928 and despatched by the SS *Andora* to Rio de Janeiro for a photographic survey. Three Vendace III trainers were delivered to Bolivia in October 1928.

The private-venture Vickers Vespa I G-EBLD built to specification 30/24 for army co-operation and powered by a Bristol Jupiter VI engine. This aircraft was also converted to the Vespa II. Six Vespa IIIs were delivered to Bolivia during 1929, and four Mk.IVs and two Mk.Vs to the Irish Air Corps in April 1930 and March 1931 respectively. The Mk.VI G-ABIL was rebuilt and converted from the Mk.I G-EBLD for a Chinese presentation and for a world height record flight after adaptation by the Bristol Aeroplane Company. The Mk.VII was G-ABIL further converted for the Royal Aircraft Establishment in May 1933 as K3588 and later used by No.4 Squadron RAF and finally, as 1051M at No.15 Technical Training School in June 1938.

The much-modified Vickers Vespa VI G-ABIL, fitted with a Bristol Pegasus 'S' (supercharged) engine, when capturing the world height record on 16 September 1932 – Britain's first-ever. Flown by Cyril Uwins, then chief test pilot of the Bristol Aeroplane Company, it reached 43,976 ft, exceeding by 800 ft the previous record held by an American navy pilot. This was a supreme example of co-operation between Rex Pierson, the aircraft designer, Roy Fedden, the engine designer, Capt Frank Barnwell, the Bristol aircraft designer who worked out the abstruse calculations, and Capt Uwins, the pilot.

The single private-venture Vickers Valiant Type 131 biplane built for the 1927 Air Ministry general-purpose aircraft competition as a D.H.9A replacement and later registered G-EBVM for demonstration in Chile where it was retained for use by the Chilian Air Force School of Aviation. Its name was to become much more famous when used again by Vickers for the first of the RAF's V-Bomber force in the 1950s.

The Vickers Wibault Scout Type 121 with braced parasol wing configuration. Developed from the French Wibault 7.C1, twenty-six were built for Chile under licence and delivered between September and November 1926. This was the first of a series of Vickers aircraft deploying the Vickers-Wibault system of construction which was based on the patents of Marcel Wibault, founder of the French aircraft company, Avions Marcel Wibault at Billancourt, Seine (from where the earlier REP patents used in the original Vickers monoplane series had emanated). Wibault became associated with Vickers as a consulting engineer in 1922 and was one of the pioneers of metal construction, his ideas closely following those of the German Junkers and Dornier companies.

The Vickers Vireo I Type 125 N211 single-seat monoplane fighter ship-plane built to Air Ministry specification 17/25 as a dual-purpose experiment to test the efficiency of the Vickers-Wibault system and to explore the operational value of a low-powered fighter for carrier-borne use at sea (and taking its name from that of a small greenish-coloured American bird). Displaying the corrugated skin of the Wibault structural concept over Brooklands, this aircraft was also flown in floatlane form.

The Vickers Viastra I G-AUUB ten-passenger commercial tri-motor monoplane transport incorporating the Vickers-Wibault structural system and intended for those underdeveloped regions where air transport would be much quicker and more economic than surface means. This aircraft was built by the recently-acquired Vickers-Supermarine, with the fuselage constructed by Vickers at Crayford, Kent. The Wibault structure essentially consisted of fabricated and corrugated light-alloy components of simple shapes and sections, thereby avoiding costly machining operations and the intricate rolled sections in sheet steel that were becoming fashionable for primary stressed members such as wing spars. It was an interesting step along the road to the sophisticated metal construction of today.

In response to interest from Australia by Sir Keith Smith of earlier Vimy fame, and then managing Vickers' aviation affairs there, two twin-engined Vickers Viastra IIs, registered VH-UOM and VH-UOO, were built by Vickers-Supermarine and shipped to West Australian Airways. The first service between Perth and Adelaide began on 3 March 1931. Although the type perfomed well, its Bristol Jupiter IXF engines were no match for the local operating conditions and the type could not fly on one engine with a full load without losing height.

The Vickers Viastra VI N-1 with a single Bristol Jupiter engine, built to another requirement of West Australian Airways but not delivered. The Viastra VIII was a further conversion of the Mk.I G-AUUB and the Viastra IX was the Mk.II VH-UOM modified for West Australian Airways by lowering the engines 15 inches on redesigned mountings, but later reconverted. The Viastra-Wallis was a special version with experimental wings in place of the Vickers-Wibault type and designed by Barnes Wallis, who had recently joined Vickers at Weybridge from the company's moribund airship works, as Chief Structures Designer to Rex Pierson. This aircraft was delivered to the RAE at Farnborough for strength tests.

The Prince of Wales alighting from the Vickers Viastra X VIP version. Registered G-ACCC on 19 December 1932, in the name of Flt Lt E.H. Fielden, the Prince's pilot (who later became the long-serving Captain of the Royal Flight) and based at Hendon, it was little used and the following year was converted by the Air Ministry as L6102 at Croydon for radio and icing tests.

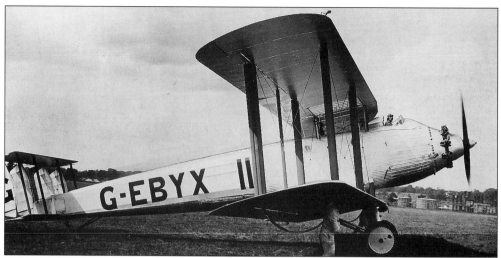

The Vickers Vellore I Type 166 G-EBYX single-engined tractor biplane civil freight and mail carrier which was first flown at Brooklands on 17 May 1928 by Scholefield and Payn. Prepared for a long-distance flight evaluation by two Australian military pilots who wished to return home, it left Brooklands on 18 March 1929 but made a forced landing at Mersa Matruh. Rebuilt by Charlie Tullett, the Vickers service engineer, aided by local Bedouin labour, it continued until suffering engine trouble 160 miles short of Darwin and crash-landed at Cape Don on 25 May 1929. The Vellore III G-AASW, built at Crayford, was evaluated with Vickers-Supermarine floats.

Using parts of the third Vellore airframe, the Vickers Vellox G-ABKY short-haul passenger carrier was first flown at Brooklands on 23 January 1934 by 'Mutt' Summers, Vickers Chief Test Pilot, and incorporated several of the modern conveniences of air travel, including individual passenger ventilation supplied by ram air from a roof intake, stressed seating with sponge rubber upholstery, soundproofed and lined cabin walls, full galley and toilet services, inertia-type engine starting, electrical instrumentation and wing and tail de-icing.

Realising at the end of 1925 that no British fighter with a liquid-cooled engine had appeared since the SE5a of First World War fame, and of which the largest number had been made by Vickers, the Type 123 private-venture (but unnamed) fighter G-EBNQ was first flown on 9 November 1926 as the first in a new line of Vickers fighter designs.

The young Fg Off Joseph 'Mutt' Summers in front of the Vickers Type 141 Scout, soon after his appointment in 1928 from Martlesham as Vickers Chief Test Pilot (after Tiny Scholefield was killed in the Vickers Vanguard biplane transport) and at the time of the Vickers takeover of Supermarine. Summers became CTP for both companies and made the first flight of the prototype Spitfire K5054 at Eastleigh on 5 March 1936. He continued to head Vickers test-flying through to the first flight of the Vickers Valiant V-Bomber in 1951 and made the first flights of thirty Vickers prototypes in his twenty-two years as Vickers Chief Test Pilot.

The Type 141 was a rebuilt version of the Type 123 with a Rolls-Royce FXI engine, a late development of the Falcon range, in place of the Hispano Suiza T52 engine which had been bought for the 123 from France through the Vickers Wibault agency. Entered for the single-seat fighter competition at Martlesham in January 1929, and later further modified as a possible deck-landing fleet fighter, it underwent sea trials onboard HMS *Furious* in June 1929. Six of the developed Type 143 were delivered to Bolivia in 1929.

The Vickers Type 177 private-venture ship-board fighter which was converted from the seventh Type 143 Bolivian Scout (of which six based on the Type 141 had been delivered between September and December 1929) and first flown by Summers at Brooklands on 26 November 1929. The Type 177 had been modified to specification F.21/26 for an Air Ministry deck-landing competition on-board HMS *Furious* in Torbay but did not prove acceptable.

The Vickers Jockey I J9122 designed by Joe Bewsher under Rex Pierson in response to Air Ministry Specification F.20/27 for an interception single-seat day fighter capable of overtaking in the shortest possible time an enemy passing overhead at 20,000 ft at a speed of 150 mph, with fighting view and manoeuvrability as primary considerations. Unusually, the name did not conform with either Vickers or Air Ministry nomenclature and is said to have been adopted to attract the French, who were using that nickname for single-seat fighters at the time.

The Vickers Venom, an improved version of the Jockey with higher perfomance for attacking faster- and higher-flying bombers. It was fitted with a 625 hp sleeve-valve Bristol Aquila engine (replacing the Mercury in the Jockey) with a hinged mounting for ease of servicing. First flown at Brooklands by 'Mutt' Summers on 17 June 1936, most of the flight trials were carried out by Flt Lt Jeffrey Quill, who had recently joined Vickers from the RAF. However, it was Reginald Mitchell's brilliant Spitfire which so effectively fulfilled this capability, and the Venom was eventually scrapped in 1939.

The Vickers Type 161 COW Gun Fighter J9596 was produced to Specification F.29/27 to carry the big 37 mm Coventry Ordnance Works (COW) gun capable of firing one-and-a-half-pounder shells in pursuit of the 'one-punch' theory of attack. It reverted to the single-seat pusher arrangement with which Vickers was earlier so familiar. First flown by Summers on 21 January 1931, it was probably the first aeroplane to use elevator trim tabs which were adjustable in flight, but was not proceeded with further.

To help keep the Weybridge production capacity busy in lean times, Vickers also built 164 Hawker Hart two-seat biplane bombers and 114 Hart Trainers between 1931 and 1936 – after building 52 Armstrong Whitworth Siskin IIIA biplane fighters, reconditioning or rebuilding 65 more, and manufacturing a large quantity of spares for this type and for the A.W. Atlas two-seater Army co-operation aircraft during 1929 and 1930.

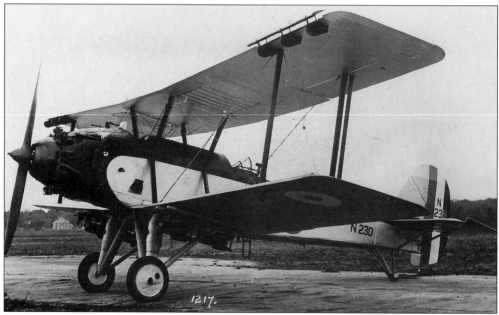

The prototype Vickers Vildebeest N230 torpedo-carrying and bombing landplane – following the Vixen/Vendace family – in its original form with a 460 hp Bristol Jupiter VIII engine. This Africaans name was suggested in September 1926 by Sir Pierre Van Ryneveld of African Vimy fame, who was then acting as the Vickers consultant in South Africa and who thought this type might engender interest there. Interestingly, it was often mispelt with a final 'e' (just as many years later conversely there were initial arguments about the final 'e' in Concorde).

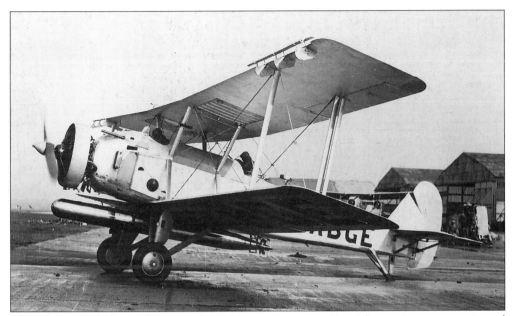

The Vickers Vildebeest I prototype N230 brought up to Spanish requirements, registered G-ABGE and designated Vickers Type 216 for demonstration to a Spanish delegation at Brooklands on 22 July 1929. A second prototype G-ABJK was also built for demonstration to the numerous other foreign governments which expressed interest.

The Vickers Vildebeest prototype G-ABGE (with SBAC symbol 0-3 which was applied initially) when fitted with Supermarine floats for demonstration to a Spanish Navy mission on Southampton Water in June 1930.

The first production Vickers Vincent K4105 at Martlesham for type tests without long-range tank but with wing-mounted bombs. The prototype Vincent S1714 was a converted Vildebeest II and was sent on an extended tour of RAF stations in the Middle East, the Sudan and East Africa on trial as a general-purpose aeroplane and with the new name because the role was quite different from that of the torpedo-bomber Vildebeest on which it was directly based. A total of 197 Vincents were built and served well in long-range tropical conditions. This was the last type to use the Vickers metal-framed construction before the inception of the Barnes Wallis geodetic-type airframe construction and the advent of Vickers' modern-type monoplane generation.

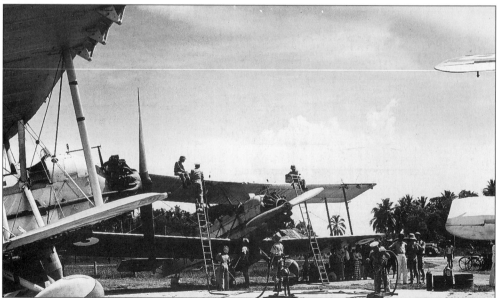

Vickers Vildebeest IIIs of 100 Squadron Royal Air Force refuelling at Kuala Lumpur. A total of 209 Vildebeest were built: two prototypes, 22 Mk.I, 30 Mk.II, 111 Mk.III, 18 Mk.IV, and 26 Mk.IX under licence in Spain for the Spanish naval air service. Thirty-seven of the Mk.IIIs and Mk.IVs were supplied to the Royal New Zealand Air Force.

Five
Canadian Vickers

In 1911, the year in which Vickers Ltd established an aviation department, at the invitation of the Canadian Government, Canadian Vickers was formed at Montreal to produce vessels for the Royal Canadian Navy; nearly three hundred ships were built during the First World War. Interest in aviation began in 1916 with various assembly and repair contracts and in 1923 a contract was won to supply eight (Vickers-Weybridge designed) Viking IV amphibians. An aircraft design staff was set up in 1924 and the first indigenous design was the Vedette three-seat seaplane, started at Weybridge and completed at Montreal by W.T. Reid, previously with Bristol; 64 were built and served the Royal Canadian Air Force until 1940. Between 1924 and 1941, 7 original designs were produced and 40 Vickers-Supermarine Stranraer flying-boats for the RCAF. Canadian Vickers also built Avro, Bellanca, Curtiss, Fairchild, Fokker and Northrop aircraft under licence. During the Second World War it also produced Handley Page Hampden fuselages for the British Government and in 1941 received a contract for the licence to build more than 300 American Consolidated PBY-5A Catalina amphibians (renamed Canso for the RCAF) and 600 PBY hulls, for which a new factory was built at Cartierville. However, in 1944 Vickers elected to withdraw from the aircraft sector to concentrate on shipbuilding, whence the company was taken over by the Canadian Government and renamed Canadair Limited.

The Weybridge-designed Vickers Viking IV Type 85 amphibian G-CYES, the first aircraft type built in Canada, and one of eight such aircraft supplied by Canadian Vickers to the Canadian Air Force (later RCAF), two of which were built at Weybridge and six at the St Hubert works of Canadian Vickers.

Four of the Canadian-built Vickers Viking IV amphibians: G-CYET, 'EY, 'EV and 'EU, ready for delivery to the Canadian Air Force.

A Canadian-built Vickers Viking IV amphibian G-CYEU patrolling over the remote Lac la Renge in 1924.

As a result of Canadian experience with the Vickers Viking IV, a smaller aeroplane was proposed for aerial survey, forestry patrol and fire-fighting. The result was the Vedette three-seat utility flying-boat, Canadian Vickers first indigenous design. The first flight, with a Rolls-Royce Falcon III engine, was made on 4 November 1924 by Flg Off W.N. Plenderleith, of the Weybridge flight test staff (who was the also the pilot of the round-the-world attempt with Sqn Ldr A.S.C. MacLaren in March 1924 with the Vickers Vulture flying-boat). The production Vedette was fitted with a Wright Whirlwind J4 engine. Sixty Vedettes were eventually built and became popular with both the RCAF and civil operators; some remained in service until the Second World War. Several also went to Chile in the first export sale of a Canadian-designed production aeroplane.

The Vickers Vedette VI G-CYWI with a Wright Whirlwind J6 engine, Handley Page-type wing leading-edge slots and a metal hull. With a span of 42 ft, length of 35 ft, a loaded weight of 4,000 lb, and speed of 111 mph, the initial rate-of-climb was 680 ft/min and the duration 5 hours. However, only this example of the Vedette VI was built.

The Canadian Vickers Varuna I G-CYGV twin-engined forestry flying-boat, powered by two Armstrong Siddeley Lynx engines, of 1927 for the Royal Canadian Air Force, and of which eight were built.

The Canadian Vickers Vista G-CYZZ flying-boat of 1927, with a single pylon-mounted Armstrong Siddeley Genet engine, of which one only was built.

The Canadian Vickers Velos G-CYYX forestry floatplane, with two Pratt and Whitney Wasp engines, intended for air survey, hence the panoramic nose crew station. Otherwise it shows a broad resemblance to the single-engined Fokker Universal and Super Universal floatplanes, also built by Canadian Vickers. With a span of 68 ft, length 44 ft and loaded weight of 7,918 lb, the speed was 85 mph. Again, only one was built, and abandoned after trials.

The Canadian Vickers Vanessa floatplane G-CYZJ of 1927 with a Wright Whirlwind J5 engine. With one crew member and up to four passengers, the span was 35 ft 3 in, length 30 ft, loaded weight 3,400 lb, maximum speed 103 mph, climb rate 550 ft/min, and the duration four-and-a-half hours. Only one was built.

The Canadian Vickers Vigil G-CYXS single-seat sesquiplane of 1928 powered by an Armstrong Siddeley Lynx engine and having a span of 35 ft 3in. Similar to the Vanessa, the length was 27 ft, loaded weight 2,250 lb and the estimated maximum speed 110 mph. Only one was built. In the background is the mooring mast used by the Vickers R.100 airship in 1930.

The Canadian Vickers Vigil G-CYXS on a shock-absorber equipped ski-type undercarriage and showing the excellent downward view for the pilot.

The Canadian Vickers Vancouver Mk.I forestries/fisheries flying-boat, the replacement for the Varuna prototype, with two Armstrong Siddeley Lynx IV engines, a span of 55 ft, length 37ft 6in, loaded weight 6,310 lb, and a maximum speed of 101 mph. The Vancouver Mk.II, of which five were built and served with the RCAF through the 1930s, had a crew of three and was fitted with geared Lynx IVC engines and had a duration of four-and-a-half hours. The Vancouver IISW was fitted with the Service-type Wright Whirlwind J6 engines and was a conversion for RCAF coastal patrol. With this sole exception, all Canadian Vickers' designs were intended for forestry patrol and associated services, such as fire suppression and air survey. The initial Vedette was much the most successful.

Of the fifty-eight Vickers-Supermarine Stranraer multi-purpose military flying-boats made, forty were licence-built by Canadian Vickers for the Royal Canadian Air Force for anti-submarine and convoy patrol duties. Fourteen were given civil registrations. This one – CF-BXO *Alaska Queen* – served with Queen Charlotte Airlines (later Pacific Western Airlines) at Vancouver during the Second World War; it is now preserved at the Royal Air Force Museum at Hendon, North London.

A Canadian Vickers-built Vickers-Supermarine Stranraer of the Royal Canadian Air Force being launched at an eastern Canadian port. When it came to deciding the shape of the fin and rudder for the Vickers B.9/32 Wellington prototype at Weybridge in 1936, 'Mutt' Summers, (Vickers CTP), liked that of the Stranraer and so it was initially adopted in enlarged form for the bomber.

Six

The Geodetic Generation

When Barnes Wallis joined Rex Pierson, Vickers Chief Designer, in 1930 at Weybridge as Chief Structures Designer, he introduced the geodetic ('basketweave') structural principle which he had developed for the retention of the gas-bags in the R.100 airship.

A geodetic line is defined as the shortest line between two points on a curved surface and is known in global navigation as a 'great circle' route. As adopted by Wallis in lattice form to aircraft structural design, it resulted in an ideal form of load-balance and fail-safe combination. In a tubular fuselage of substantially single curvature, two helices running in opposite directions were stabilised by quartile longerons and joined at each intersection so that one set of members was in tension while the other was in compression; the curved diagonal lattice-work (along the lines in which the principal in-flight forces acted) absorbed all loads by stress equalization. The resulting structural system replaced the conventional primary and secondary members with a system of main members only, which was self-stabilising and did the work of the shell of a normal monocoque without the need for an internal load-carrying structure. It also dispensed with the need for stressed-skinning, and fabric covering was used. The chief advantages were the ability to adopt a near-ideal streamlined shape while simultaneously providing maximum unobstructed internal space.

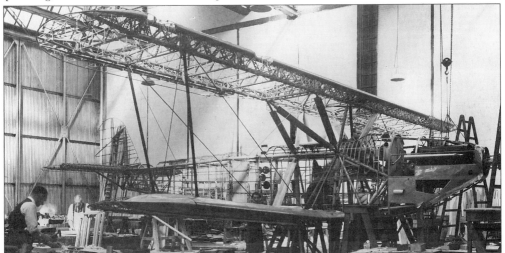

The Vickers M.1/30 Type 207 torpedo-bomber ship-plane replacement prototype being assembled in October 1932 at Weybridge with its close structural affinity to airship practice in the wing spars. Incorporated by Barnes Wallis, designer of the Vickers R.100 airship, who had joined Rex Pierson at Weybridge in 1930, this was effectively the birth of the geodetic generation of Vickers aircraft featuring his unique geodetic ('basketweave') type of airframe structure.

The Rolls-Royce 825 hp Buzzard-powered Vickers M.1/30 S1641 running up at Brooklands before its first test flight on 11 January 1933 by 'Mutt' Summers with John Radcliffe as his flight observer. After twenty-four test flights, they took-off on 23 November 1933 to carry out ceiling and level speed trials at full load when the aircraft broke up during a high-speed dive but both crew survived. The RAE investigation deduced that the accident was probably caused by a disorted tailplane incidence jack resulting in excessive force being exerted on the wings and tail. Their findings resulted in the complete rewriting of the tail structure stress formulae in the official Air Ministry publication A.P 970 on design calculations.

The Vickers G.4/31 K2771 general purpose bombing and torpedo biplane prototype at Brooklands prior to it being first flown solo there by Summers on 16 August 1934. Undeterred by the loss of the Vickers M.1/30, Barnes Wallis had greatly extended the application of his geodetic principle in this succeeding Vickers aircraft type.

The Vickers G.4/31 biplane prototype over Brooklands before trials by the RAE at Farnborough and the official tests at Martlesham, and before the private-venture Vickers Type 246 monoplane version to the same specification was flown by Summers for the first time at Brooklands on 19 June 1935. When rejected in favour of the Vickers PV monoplane, K2771 was eventually retained by the Bristol Aeroplane Company at Filton until the war as a flying test-bed.

The prototype Vickers G.4/31 monoplane with a complete geodetic-type airframe structure under construction at Weybridge. Its biplane counterpart is in the background and, on the left, a Bristol Pegasus engine and former for the mock-up of the later Vickers B.9/32 Wellington bomber prototype.

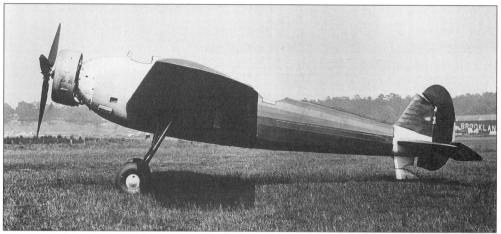

The substantially better performing private-venture Vickers G.4/31 Wellesley prototype monoplane K7556 which was first flown at Brooklands by Summers on 19 June 1935. Even with orders for 150 aircraft, Sir Robert McLean, the forceful Chairman of Vickers (Aviation) Ltd, believing that the G.4/31 biplane specification was too pedestrian, told the Air Ministry, 'I suggest to you that it might be better to reduce these orders in numbers and in their place go into production of the monoplane as soon as tooling can be completed. Meantime, and until you can decide whether we shall be allowed to switch over from the biplane to the monoplane, I do not wish to proceed with work on the biplane because, in my view, it is not a modern machine'.

The fourteenth production Vickers Wellesley K7726 long-range monoplane bomber over Southern England. The black-and-white markings along the line of the wing spars are footprints for ground staff to use when walking on the fabric-covered geodetic surface. A total of 177 Wellesleys was built, including the prototype K7556.

Ground preparation of the three Vickers Wellesleys – L2638 (Sqn Ldr R. Kellett), L2639 (Flt Lt H.A.V. Hogan) and L2680 (Flt Lt A.N. Combe) which were converted for the specially-formed Royal Air Force Long Range Development Unit (LRDU), seen here before their successful attempt on the world long-distance record. Leaving Ismailia in Egypt on 5 November 1938 and landing at Darwin in Northern Australia on 7 November 1938 (significantly at the airfield named after Ross Smith, commander of the famous Vickers Vimy England-to-Australia flight of nineteen years earlier), Kellett and Combe completed the flight to create the record which was homolgated by the FAI as 7,158.653 miles (11,520.421 kilometres) at an average speed of 149 mph. It stood for eight years until 1946.

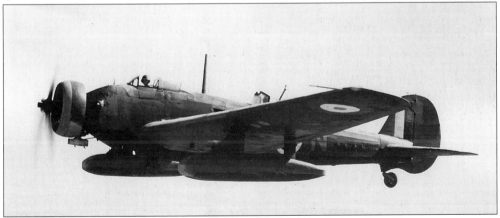

A Vickers Wellesley during an air raid on Keren during the Italian East African campaign in 1940. Wellesleys began service with the RAF in 1937 in England and the Middle East. When they were replaced in RAF Bomber Command in 1939 by Vickers Wellingtons and other types, they were transferred to Middle East Command and served well in the early stages of the Second World War – notably in the attack launched from Aden on Italian Somaliland, as well as in the Desert War in North Africa.

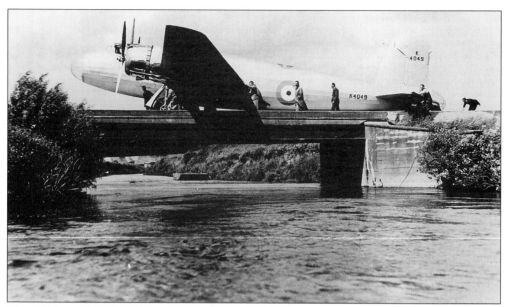

The Vickers B.9/32 Wellington prototype K4049 being rolled across the River Wey at Brooklands, at that time on private property, the landowner charging a toll for all aircraft except those bearing roundels and signifying Air Ministry ownership. The first flight was made there by Summers on 15 June 1936, during which he was accompanied by Barnes Wallis, who was responsible for the airframe structure, and Trevor Westbrook, who was transferred to Weybridge from Vickers-Supermarine to bring the complex geodetic system into full-scale production.

The nose and forward fuselage of the Vickers B.9/32 prototype bomber, before fabric covering and showing the complex detail of the Wallis geodetic construction and the cupola-type windshield for the front gunner.

Wellington Development

The Vickers Wellington bomber is the best known of all the Vickers aeroplanes conceived by the company's renowned Chief Designer, Rex Pierson, and affectionately remembered as the 'Wimpy' by Royal Air Force and Allied airmen of many nationalities. After curiously being briefly named *Crecy*, as well as being officially named after a town according to Air Ministry nomenclature, and perpetuating the memory of the Iron Duke, in popular public perception it was named after the cartoon character Popeye's stout hamburger-devouring friend, J.Wellington Wimpy, featured in the famous strip-cartoon in the *Daily Mirror* and, with no coincidence, linked to the German port of Hamburg which was suffering more than a little from the Vickers bomber at the time.

The Wellington appeared in many roles in every theatre of the Second World War, serving with every Command of the RAF, except Fighter, and eight Commonwealth airforces. It formed the backbone of RAF Bomber Command in the early years of the war, until the advent of the four-engined 'heavies'; participating in the first aerial attack – on 4 September 1939 – the Wellington later provided 599 of the 1,043 aircraft in the first 'Thousand Bomber' raid. From September 1940, it was a front-line bomber in the Middle East right through until the end of the war. It was adaptable, also appearing in diverse other roles: minesweeping, electronic countermeasures, crew training, civil transport, jet engine development and pressure cabin research. The Wellington was utimately retired from service at the end of March 1953, having also provided the basis for the Vickers Viking, Britain's first post-war airliner.

The Wellington prototype K4049, designed to Air Ministry specification B.9/32 was first flown on 15 June 1936 by 'Mutt' Summers, Vickers famous Chief Test Pilot, from the Brooklands airfield at Weybridge, where it had been built. The promise of its excellent aerodynamics and high-strength lightweight structure prompted an order of 180 aircraft of a re-engined version to Specification B.29/36, two months after this first flight. Unfortunately, this historic aircraft was destroyed when it crashed due to elevator imbalance near the end of its trials at the Aeroplane and Armament Experimental Establishment (A&AEE) at Martlesham Heath, Suffolk.

Contrary to popular assumption, the production Wellington incorporated improvements from the design of its bigger, heavier and more capacious sibling Vickers aeroplane, the B.1/35 (which eventually became the Warwick and followed the Wellington in production at Weybridge). The two types were generally similar, but the Wellington had a shorter fuselage, smaller inner wings, but identical outers. From the initial flight of the first production aircraft on 23 December 1937, 11,461 Wellingtons were eventually built – 2,515 at Weybridge and 5,540 and 3,406 at the government-owned Shadow Factories at Chester (Hawarden) and Blackpool (Squire's Gate) respectively – an average rate of thirty-one-and-a-half per month for seven years and two weeks.

The Wellington's geodetic structure provided a difficult production challenge and great credit is due to Trevor Westbrook, the Weybridge General Manager and his team for its ultimate success.

Sixteen basic Marks of Wellington were produced, using four basic engine types: the Bristol Pegasus and Hercules, the Pratt and Whitney Twin Wasp and the Rolls-Royce Merlin; the Type was developed in weight from the 24,800 lb of the Pegasus XVIII-powered Mk.1, via the 31,600 lb of the Twin-Wasp R1830-powered Mk.IV, to the 36,500 lb of the Hercules XVII-powered Mk.XVIII, and in speed from 245 mph to the 300 mph of the Merlin 60-powered pressurised high-altitude bomber version.

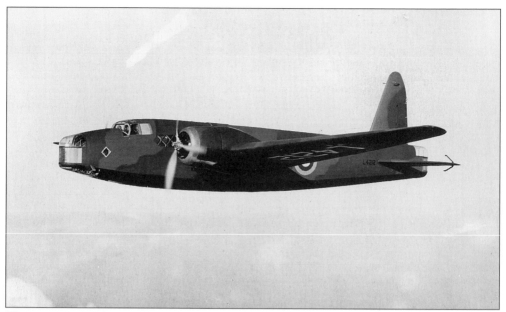

The prototype Vickers Wellington Mk.I L4212, a substantial redesign from the B.9/32, which made its first flight at Brooklands on 23 December 1937. Powered by two Bristol Pegasus XVIII engines with de Havilland-Hamilton Standard two-pitch propellers, it incorporated bow and stern power-operated gun turrets plus a ventral retractable turret amidships, all of Vickers' design.

Quantity production of Vickers Wellington I geodetic fuselages in the erecting shop at Weybridge.

Wellington fuselages, with inner planes and engine nacelles fitted, passing tightly-packed down the Weybridge assembly line.

The Vickers Wellington IC P9349 powered by two 1,050 hp Bristol Pegasus engines, equipped with Frazer-Nash gun turrets, built at Weybridge and delivered to the Royal Air Force in January 1940.

A typical scene on a wartime Royal Air Force Bomber Command station: a Vickers Wellington IC of No.149 Squadron bombing up and refuelling.

The Vickers Wellington Mk.X HE239 after returning from a raid on the German industrial city of Duisburg in April 1943, showing the extraordinary robustness of the geodetic airframe structure and its ability to withstand severe battle damage while still maintaining sufficient residual strength and airworthiness to get home.

A Vickers Wellington Mk.II powered by two 1,145 hp Rolls-Royce Merlin engines and used for the night-bombing offensive in the European theatre of war.

The converted Vickers Wellington DWI Mk.I HX682 fitted with a 48 ft diameter duralumin degaussing ring for operation as a destroyer of the German magnetic mines which posed such a threat to British shipping. Energised by either a Ford V8 or a de Havilland Gypsy Six engine, the twelve Wellington DWI conversions so equipped were successfully used in the Thames estuary, the Suez Canal, Mediterranean harbours and later, in the Near East, until degaussing gear had been fitted to ships. George Edwards, who had joined the Vickers' design team at Weybridge in 1935, was given the task of running the design and manufacture of this device in continuous working over the 1939 Christmas period. Such was the urgency of the conversion of the prototype P2516 that he had to send a set of progress photographs every night to the First Lord of the Admiralty, then Winston Churchill. Designated Directional Wireless Installation (DWI) deliberately to confuse the enemy, in the workshops it was known as 'Down With 'Itler'.

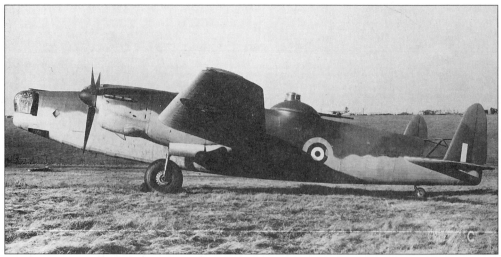

The Vickers Wellington Mk.II prototype L4250 (the thirty-eighth production airframe) in twin-fin layout for in-flight firing trials of the mid-upper turret-mounted 40 mm cannon and for which the centre fuselage was modified to take a stressed-skin section. The whole installation was assembled at Weybridge under the supervision of Capt Naninni of Vickers House, with other Vickers' subsidiary companies providing specialist components and support.

The prototype Bristol Hercules-powered Vickers Wellington Mk.V Type 407 R3298 high-altitude stratosphere bomber development, with its pressurised crew compartment in position, and intended for operation between 35,000 and 40,000 ft above the ceiling of enemy fighters. This installation entailed marrying a pressure vessel to a geodetic-type airframe, theoretically a contradiction in terms. The cabin was therefore attached by integral feet anchored to the nodal points of the structure, thus allowing it to expand and contract independent of the rest of the airframe. The design and flying trials of the two prototypes, R3298 and R3299, provided the basis for all British aircraft pressure cabin installations, the Vickers-Supermarine Spitfire and the Westland Welkin being the first in which the experience was applied. Nine Wellington Vs were built.

The prototype Rolls-Royce Merlin 60-powered Wellington Mk.VI Type 431 W5795 of which thirty-two were built and intended for experiments with the 'Oboe' blind bombing aid. However, changing military policies resulted in the high-altitude bombing requirement being adequately filled by developments of the de Havilland Mosquito, with oxygen but not a pressure cabin, which could outperform the Wellington at height. Experience with the Wellington V and VI was to be of great value to Vickers in the design of the post-war Viscount turboprop airliner and the Valiant jet bomber.

The prototype Royal Air Force Coastal Command Vickers Wellington Mk.VIII W5674, completed at Weybridge with Bristol Pegasus engines for trials with fuselage spine-mounted ASV (Air-to-Surface Vessel) radar antennae and developed into a major weapon against the German U-boat menace in the Battle of the Atlantic. Success was later achieved with a combination of a Leigh-type searchlight, in place of the nose turret, and the ASV radar synchronised with the actual dropping of bombs, depth charges or torpedoes. This combination made it possible to track a vessel at sea in complete darkness before mounting a surprise attack with a powerful instant illumination of the moving target.

The Royal Air Force Coastal Command Vickers Wellington Mk.XIII with chin-mounted ASV radar.

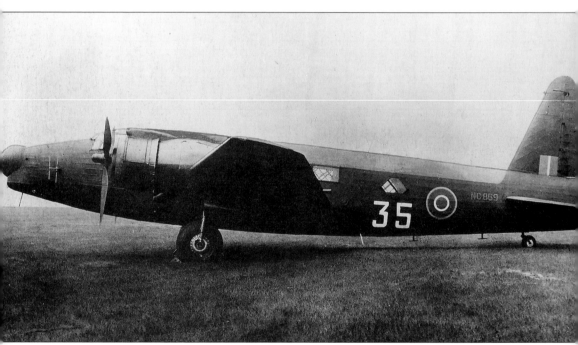

A Bristol Hercules-powered, Blackpool-built, Vickers Wellington Mk.T XVIII NC869 (conversion from a Mk.XI) with a de Havilland Mosquito night-fighter nose but no tail turret, used as a Mk.XVII trainer.

The hybrid Vickers Wellington Mk.II with Rolls-Royce Merlin X engines, used as a flying test-bed aircraft for the pioneering Whittle jet engine mounted in the fuselage tail – the first instance of a rear-mounted jet engine which was to come into widespread use in the post-war years, notably by Vickers with the VC10 and the British Aircraft Corporation with the BAC One-Eleven. Three Wellington Mk.IIs – Z8570, W5389 and W5518 – were converted at Weybridge in 1942 and 1943, and between 1944 and 1945 at least 15 types of early jet engines were evaluated in these high-flying test-bed aircraft with a total of 512 hours logged in 366 flights.

A Whittle-designed, 2,500 lb thrust, Power Jets W2/700 pure jet engine mounted in the tail of the Vickers Wellington II W5518, a hybrid aircraft with Mk.VI wings and Merlin XX engines which reached 36,000 ft but could not maintain level flight on the jet engine alone. The 'ear' type air intakes were flush-mounted on the rear end of the fuselage sides.

The Pratt and Whitney Double Wasp-powered Vickers Warwick ASR (Air-Sea Rescue) Mk.I carrying a lifeboat in 1943. Originally designed to Air Ministry Specification B.1/35, the Warwick actually gave birth to the smaller and much more successful Wellington as they were being designed in parallel – but which it eventually followed in production. Fortunately, the frustrated development of the Warwick for the bomber role, mainly due to engine problems, was compensated by its spacious fuselage and long range; this later led to worthwhile roles in the ASR, GR (general reconnaissance), troop/freight-carrying and civil transport. The full complement of 845 Warwicks was built at Weybridge.

A fully-rigged Warwick Mk.II airborne lifeboat designed by Uffa Fox, the well-known yacht designer and racer. This single-engined 30 ft boat weighing 3,600 lb was released from the aircraft's bomb-bay supported by two 96 ft parachutes, in comparison to the earlier twin-engined 27 ft Mk.I boat which was supported by six 32 ft parachutes. Wind-tunnel dropping tests of a one-fifteenth scale model of the Warwick lifeboat by the Royal Aircraft Establishment were satisfactory and showed no tendency for it to roll over; both types were widely and successfully deployed in service by the ASR Warwick.

The Vickers Warwick C.Mk.I G-AGFK, the last of fourteen aircraft converted for British Overseas Airways Corporation (BOAC) in 1943 for the carriage of mail, freight and passengers (in that order of priority) across Africa between Bathhurst in West Africa and Cairo, to complement the airline's flying-boat operation between England and Bathurst. Passenger windows, exhaust-stack flame-dampers and faired-over gun turret positions characterised this conversion from the B.Mk.I bomber version.

The Vickers Warwick C.III troop and freight transport developed directly from the B.Mk.I bomber version and fitted with a large under-fuselage pannier in place of the bomb compartment for carrying military equipment or long-range tanks. However, heat-cracking of the wing top surfaces prevented the type being used in the Far East and it was thus confined to the RAF Transport Command mail and freight service between the UK and Athens via Naples from early 1945 until March 1946.

The first protoytype Vickers Windsor at Farnborough at the time of its first flight by 'Mutt' Summers on 23 October 1943, having been assembled in a specially-built hangar later used by the Empire Test Pilots' School. The Windsor had its origins in the Air Ministry Specification B.12/36 for a four-engined long-range heavy bomber, the same requirement to which Reginald Mitchell of Vickers-Supermarine produced his highly-promising but regrettably last design. The Windsor eventually materialised in response to Specification B.3/42 with two prototypes, DW506 and DW512, powered by four Rolls-Royce Merlin 60 engines, with an elliptical wing (as in Mitchell's moribund design) and four Wellington-type twin-oleo undercarriage units, one in each engine nacelle.

The Vickers Windsor DW506 which, after 33 hrs 45 mins flying time, force-landed at Grove airfield, Wantage, on 2 March 1944, breaking its back. For structural efficiency, the wing geometry was designed to have a defined droop so that under in-flight loads it became straight. Geodetic construction was again used but with the geometrical pattern arranged to suit the critical wing loadings (similar to directional tape-laying in today's carbon-fibre structures). Geodetic members ran across the wing at 45 degrees for torsional stiffness outboard, and at 16 degrees to the spanwise direction inboard, to manage the heavy bending loads; several ingenious skin coverings were also tried. Intended for use against Japan, the 300-aircraft Windsor programme was cancelled when the war ended.

Seven

The Shadows
and Dispersals of War

The demands of the Royal Air Force Expansion Scheme during the late 1930s to meet the needs of another impending conflict in Europe and the daunting prospect of bringing the complex geodetic-type structural design of the Wellington into high-volume output, required a completely new production concept and supplier network.

The introduction of the brilliant Trevor Westbrook from Vickers-Supermarine, who had already played a dynamic role in putting into production the advanced all-metal Spitfire airframe, resulted in the manufacture of the vast range of individual geodetic members being accomplished with ingenious Weybridge-designed, multi-cam controlled, drawbench machines. The two government-owned, Vickers-operated, Shadow Factories at Chester and Blackpool then augmented the parent plant at Weybridge. A major setback came in September 1940 with devastating bombing raids on the Weybridge plant and on Vickers-Supermarine at Southampton. The rapid dispersal of Wellington manufacture into nearly ninety small local sites and the reactivation of the Weybridge factory was exemplary.

Wellington production was thus sustained throughout the war, producing 11,461 aircraft in what was Britain's most prolific and successful two-motor military bomber aircraft programme. This was complemented at Weybridge with 845 of the bigger Warwick.

The Vickers Type 432 F.7/41 DZ217 'Metal Mossie' high-speed twin-engined fighter built in the early part of the Second World War and for which Barnes Wallis devised Vickers first true stressed-skin structure. Built in two halves, the wings were joined at the leading and trailing edges and known as 'pea-pod' or 'lobster claw' construction. This single prototype was first flown at Farnborough on 24 December 1942 by Vickers test pilot Tommy Lucke but the programme was abandoned in May 1943 in favour of the all-wooden de Havilland Mosquito. This aircraft was retained by Vickers for flight control evaluations for the Vickers Windsor geodetic bomber.

The Vickers-Weybridge factory shortly before the disastrous German bombing raid of 4 September 1940. Well-known in both international motorsport and aviation circles, despite gallant attempts to camouflage the Brooklands motor-racing track and factory buildings, fourteen Junkers Ju88 dive bombers attacked the factory. Although the attack occurred during the lunch break, 84 work-people were killed with another 300 injured. An immediate and widespread dispersal of Wellington production was made to nearly ninety small units in the local area and the main assembly plant was quickly re-established.

The Vickers Wellington Mk.IC production line at Weybridge. When enemy air raids threatened, a system of heavy wooden struts was installed to support the erecting shop roof against collapse from bomb blast damage. These struts were arranged between the roof gantry main support points and the factory floor during the daytime; they were hinged and swung into the roof each night to facilitate moving the airframes forward for the next stage of assembly the following day.

Vickers Wellington geodetic wing panel assembly at the 32,000 sq ft floor space dispersal unit at Twickenham Film Studios.

Vickers Wellington geodetic wing panel assembly at the 25,000 sq ft floor space dispersal unit at the Oriental Works at Woking.

Left: Assembly of the complex yet highly-efficient and durable geodetic-type structure of the Vickers Wellington. Most commendably, nearly half of the workforce were women. Right: Trevor Westbrook, General Manager of the Vickers-Weybridge, Chester and Blackpool factories and Wellington production supervisor during the early part of the war. It is to him that much of the credit must go for bringing the geodetic-type construction to full-scale, high-rate production.

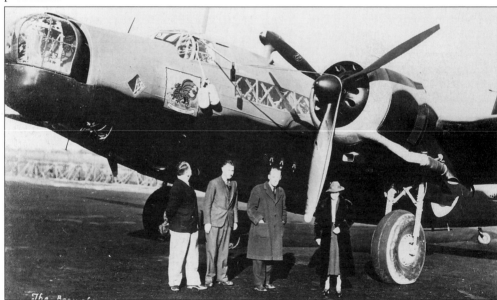

The naming of *The Broughton Wellington* Mk.IC R1333 on 7 November 1940, which was built at the huge government-owned, Vickers-Armstrongs-managed Shadow Factory at Chester, actually in North Wales and also known as Hawarden (pronounced 'Harden'), the name of the airfield, or Broughton, the name of the nearby village. It was given to the Royal Air Force by the Chester workforce (with the Bristol Aeroplane Company workforce giving the Pegasus engines). Left to right are: Tommy Lucke (Vickers Test Pilot); Gordon Montgomery (works manager); Bernard Duncan (general manager), and Miss Scott, a senior secretary who had worked at Vickers House in London before the war, and who cut the ribbon.

Vickers Wellington final assembly at the Vickers-operated Shadow Factory at Chester where (together with a secondary assembly line at Byley on the perimeter of Cranage aerodrome, near Middlewich) a total 5,540 Wellingtons – three Mk.I; 17 Mk.IA; 1,583 Mk.IC; 737 Mk.III; 220 Mk.IV; 2,434 Mk.X; 8 Trolicalised MkXII, and 538 Mk.XIV – were built between 1939 and 1944; 235 Avro Lancaster B.Is were also delivered between June 1944 and September 1945.

The 1,000th Vickers Wellington ready for delivery at the Vickers-operated Shadow Factory at Blackpool in 1942. Left to right: Frank White (subcontract manager); Les Webb (production manager); Pat Molony (works manager); Sam Bower (general manager); Ernie Comley (personnel manager), and Teddy Major (chief inspector). A total of 3,406 Wellingtons – 50 Mk.IC; 780 Mk.III; 1,369 Mk.X; 75 Mk.XI; 802 Mk.XIII; 250 Mk.XIV; and 80 Mk. XVIII – were built between 1940 and 1945. After the war ended, both the Chester and Blackpool factories each built 11,250 AIROH (Aircraft Industry Research on Housing) prefabricated houses between September 1945 and April 1948 before these two factories were taken over by de Havilland and Hawker respectively, to resume aircraft production.

The Battle of Britain Memorial Flight (BBMF) Avro Lancaster B.I PA474 which was built by Vickers at Chester in 1945. After photographic reconnaissance duties in East and South Africa, it was transferred to the College of Aeronautics at Cranfield, Bedfordshire, for trials of the Handley Page laminar flow wing until 1964 when it was adopted by the Air Historical Branch and took part in two films before being restored for flying display with the BBMF, which it joined in November 1973. It was adopted by the City of Lincoln in 1975. During the winter of 1995/6, this historic Vickers-built Lancaster received a new main spar to extend its flying life well into the next millennium.

The other important Vickers association with the Avro Lancaster heavy-bomber was the highly original Barnes Wallis-designed *Upkeep* bouncing bomb that was deployed by 617 Squadron Royal Air Force Lancasters on 16/17 May 1943 in the famous 'Dambusters' raid on the German industrial Ruhr valley. The weapon itself was 4 ft 11.5 in wide, 4 ft 2 in diameter and had 6,000 lb of RDX explosive filling. Suspended in the bomb-bay from two V-shaped arms, a chain drive from a motor inside the fuselage spun the bomb backwards at 500 rpm before it was dropped at a height of only 60 ft to bounce across the water surface and, skipping over anti-torpedo netting, roll down the dam wall before exploding to exert massive water pressure to breach the masonry.

Eight

The Post-War Progression: Britain's First to Biggest

The post-war Vickers progression of large civil and military aircraft ranged from Britain's first, to biggest, with a span of technology that was unique in the Western World.

The Viking was Britain's first post-war airliner and a jet conversion was the world's first airliner to be powered exclusively by turbine power. From the Viking stemmed the military Valetta and Varsity derivatives. The Viscount was the world's first turbine-powered airliner to carry fare-paying passengers and pioneered the benefits of this exciting new mode of air transport throughout the world.

The Valiant was the first British V-bomber and a pioneer in the development of Britain's atomic weapons and of in-flight refuelling with large military jet aircraft. Although the low-cost Vanguard turboprop airliner was overtaken by the jets, it did introduce important new technical innovations and latterly served well in the cargo business.

Again, although curtailed by the vacillating policies of BOAC in the procurement of British versus American aircraft, the VC10 intercontinental jetliner was Britain's largest aircraft ever to enter series production and was extremely popular before adaptation to its strategic military roles of today. Paradoxically, the ill-fated TSR-2 supersonic bomber proved to be the catalyst of the formation of the British Aircraft Corporation with the Vickers team as the leading partner. The crowning achievements of the original Vickers aviation team were then the development of the BAC One-Eleven regional jetliner and its major share in the Anglo-French Concorde programme.

The prototype Vickers Viking VC1 (Vickers Commercial One), Britain's first post-war airliner and appropriately-registered G-AGOK, running up before its first flight by 'Mutt' Summers, from Wisley airfield on 22 June 1945 (with a Warwick GR.Mk.V from which it derived its tail surfaces in the background). The Viking was developed by Rex Pierson, as a civil derivative of his wartime Wellington bomber and as a temporary interim machine until the Brabazon Committee recommendations for wholly-new civil aircraft could be implemented.

Final assembly of the twenty-one-seat Vickers Viking airliner series at Weybridge. With a Wellington geodetic-type wing, engine nacelles and undercarriage, the Viking was powered by Bristol Hercules radial engines. The major change was its spacious stressed-skin monocoque-type fuselage, Vickers first, incorporated fifteen years after the primary American manufacturers were able to do so. The Viking was also the first post-war design to comply with the new International Civil Aviation Organisation (ICAO) performance regulations.

The Vickers Viking Mk.IA G-AIVB *Vernal* of the type which began service on 1 September 1946 with the British European Airways Corporation (BEA), formed a month earlier under the Civil Aviation Act 1946. On that day, the BEA Viking G-AHOP *Valerie* left Northolt, then serving as London's continental airport, for Kastrup, Copenhagen, so epitomising its type name. BEA eventually operated 83 Vikings. The ex-BEA Viking IA G-AGRU *Vagrant*, also in the original BEA Keyline markings, and the only surviving Vickers Viking in the UK, is now on display at the Brooklands Museum at Weybridge.

The 'Long-Nose' Vickers Viking IB G-AJJN Type 336 24-27 seat company demonstrator which flew to New Zealand in April 1947, returning in June, having covered a total distance of 40,000 miles. It was then used to initiate a Vickers communications flight at Wisley, subsequently being sold to BEA. A total of 163 Vikings were built, many being exported for both airline and government VIP use; a few were still flying in the early 1970s.

Among the many uses to which the Viking was put was the re-introduction of the King's Flight, and it was used for the royal tour of South Africa in 1947. This is the Royal Flight of specially-appointed Vikings – VL245, VL246 and VL247 (the workshop support aircraft) – about to embark the royal party at Bloemfontein airport for a flight to the Orange Free State game reserve on 13 March 1947.

The first of five Vickers Vikings OY-DLA of DDL (Danish Air Lines) of Copenhagen – the Viking homeland and thus named *Tor Viking*.

The Vickers Viking Type 649 J750 Pakistan Air Force Government executive aircraft.

The Vickers Nene-Viking Type 618 VX856/G-AJPH, a converted Ministry of Supply aircraft, powered by two Rolls-Royce Nene turbojets, in place of the standard Bristol Hercules 634 engines. This was the world's first airliner to be powered exclusively by jet propulsion. First flown by Summers from Wisley on 6 April 1948, on 25 July 1948 he flew it from London Airport to Villacoublay, Paris, in the record time of 34 min 7 sec at an average speed of 384 mph, which still compares favourably with today's jets.

The Vickers Valetta C.Mk.1 VW141, one of the 263 such aircraft which became the 'workhorse' of airborne combined operations. Developed as a multi-role military transport aircraft to specification C.9/46 as a result of the successful operation of the Vickers Viking by Royal Air Force Transport Command, the Valetta was widely used as a troop carrier, VIP transport, military freighter, ambulance, glider-tug, paratroop transport and for supply dropping. Described as five-aeroplanes-in-one, the concept of all-round transport utility, originally born in the Middle East and India with the Vickers biplane transports, had at last received due recognition and was to be greatly developed in the RAF VC10.

A para-dropping Vickers Valetta with the exit door fitted within an enlarged two-part, sideways-opening, freight-loading door – which could also be used with skewed ground ramps for drive-in loading of light military vehicles and artillery. The truncated fuselage tail-cone was to accommodate formation lights and a glider-towing attachment (which was directly linked to a heavy triangulated structure inside the rear fuselage to transfer the towing loads to the airframe primary structure).

A Valetta T.Mk.4 WJ471 radar trainer distinguished by its radar scanner-equipped longer-nose and of which eighteen aircraft were converted. The flying navigational classroom Valetta T.Mk.3 to specification T.1/49 had ten student training positions and was used by the Air Navigation School at Hullavington and the RAF College at Cranwell, the distinguishing feature being the row of transparent, fuselage spine-mounted, astrodomes.

The prototype Vickers Varsity multi-engined military crew trainer Type 668 VX828 lifting-off on its first flight by Summers at Wisley on 17 July 1949 (a year-and-a-day after the first flight of the Vickers Viscount turboprop airliner). The Varsity, the last Vickers piston-engined (Bristol Hercules 264) aircraft, was built to Specification T.13/48 which was written to cover this imaginative specialised design submitted by Vickers as the ultimate development of the Viking and Valetta family, also incorporating Viscount-type petal engine-cowlings and tricycle undercarriage.

The prototype Vickers Varsity Type 668 VX828 with the distinguishing feature of a ventral pannier accommodating the V-bomber type bomb-aimer's prone position and used in conjunction with twenty-four 25 lb practice bombs. Mudguards had to be fitted to the nosewheels to keep the sighting window clear – as also later became necessary on the Vickers Valiant jet bomber.

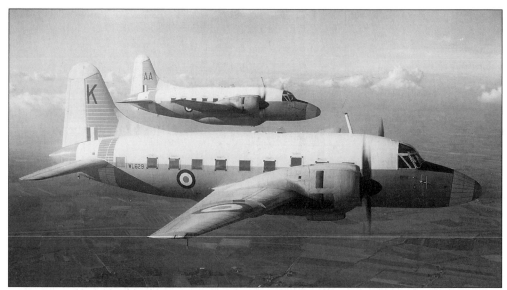

Vickers Varsity T.MkIs WL629 and WL627 of No.5 Flight Training School Royal Air Force Oakington, Cambridgeshire. Of the 163 Varsitys built, the first 17 were made at Weybridge and the remaining 146 at the Vickers satellite plant at Hurn (Bournemouth) airport, which was established in 1951 to provide additional capacity to relieve Weybridge at the time of the anticipated large-scale production build-up there. The Varsity WF372, the sixteenth aircraft built at Weybridge, which served with the RAF for 25 years until 1976, is now displayed in RAF Training Command colours of the 1960s at the Brooklands Museum at Weybridge.

The Vickers Varsity VX835 powered by Napier Eland turboprop engines and fitted with a spray rig for the engine icing clearance tests to British Air Registration Board (ARB) and American Federal Aviation Agency (FAA) requirements which were carried out in 1957/58, the aircraft being operated from the Napier factory at Luton and at Cranfield, Bedfordshire.

Vickers Varsity T.Mk.I WL679 research aircraft used by the Royal Aircraft Establishment (RAE) at Bedford and later based at RAE Farnborough. This aircraft was the last airworthy example of the type, until its retirement in August 1991 and being flown to the Cosford Aerospace Museum for preservation. Civil conversion WF387/G-ARFP was used for automatic landing with Smiths Aviation Division; WF415/G-APAZ for radar and navigation systems research with Decca and WF416/VK-510 for the personal use of King Hussein of Jordan.

The Vickers Wellington Mk.X LN715 fitted with Rolls-Royce Dart turboprop engines and converted at Hucknall, Nottinghamshire, as a test-bed prefacing the installation of the Dart in the Viscount airliner.

The original prototype Vickers Viscount VC2 Type 630 G-AHRF ('Roger Fox') taking off from Wisley on its first flight on 16 July 1948 in unpainted exterior and in the hands of 'Mutt' Summers, partnered by Gabe ('Jock') Bryce, who had joined Vickers from the Kings Flight and who succeeded Summers in 1951. What was to prove to be another defining moment in British and world civil aviation, this pioneering aeroplane had been conceived by Rex Pierson, in response to the wartime Brabazon Committee IIB requirement as a replacement for the interim Vickers Viking.

The diminutive (32-passenger) Vickers Viscount 630 G-AHRF in the colours of British European Airways (BEA) with its distinctive forward-mounted 1,380 hp Rolls-Royce Dart propeller-turbine engines. It was the harbinger of a whole new air passenger experience throughout the world with a new sound in the sky and vibration-free, 'over-the-weather', pressurised and air-conditioned passenger comfort.

The Vickers Tay Viscount Type 663 with the service serial VX217, the second prototype Viscount airframe converted to a flying test-bed for the Rolls-Royce Tay pure jet engine (developed from the Nene which had been similarly-tested in the Vickers Viking) and the world's first aircraft to fly with an electrically-signalled (fly-by-wire) flight-control system. First flown on 15 March 1950, the Tay Viscount was subsequently used by Boulton Paul for the development of electrically-signalled flying controls for the Vickers Valiant four-jet bomber and thus pioneered the universal use of fly-by-wire controls in today's civil and military aircraft.

The world's first scheduled, fare-paying, turbine-powered air transport passengers boarding the Viscount 630 G-AHRF on 29 July 1950 to fly from London to Paris. This service continued for two weeks before the aircraft operated on the London-Edinburgh route between 15 August and 23 August 1950, the period of the Edinburgh Festival; 1,815 passengers were carried during the two operations in a total of 127 flying hours. In this way, the determined combination of George Edwards, who had succeeded Rex Pierson as Vickers Chief Designer, and Peter Masefield, Chief Executive of BEA, rescued the Viscount from near still-birth in the face of a cooling of interest in the boldness which the Viscount heralded.

Frank Whittle, the world-famous inventor of the jet engine (left) and George Edwards (right), the world-renowned mentor of the Vickers Viscount as well as the entire Vickers post-war jet-age aircraft progression, together in the Viscount 630, experiencing and demonstrating the extraordinarily smooth, vibration-free passenger ride by balancing a lead pencil on end, a contemporary twelve-sided threepenny bit on edge and observing a ripple-free glass of wine on the passenger table. Two of Britain's and the world's finest engineers, both were later knighted and awarded the exclusive Order of Merit (OM) at the personal discretion of the Queen.

George Edwards (centre), when Vickers Chief Designer, in characteristic stance with three of his most senior technical colleagues. Left to right: Hugh Hemsley (aerodynamics and flight test), Ernie Marshall (projects) and Basil Stephenson (structures).

The Vickers Viscount Rolls-Royce Dart propeller-turbine (outer) engine and nacelle with the firewall and tubular W-strut mounting structure completely ahead of the uninterrupted main wing structure and petal-type cowlings affording all-round access to the engine and accessories in the pencil-slim nacelle.

The prototype Vickers Viscount Type 700 G-AMAV, first flown from Brooklands by 'Jock' Bryce, on 28 August 1950, a month after the world's first passenger-carrying services with the Type 630. It is here in tropical surroundings when being flown by a BEA team led by the airline's chief executive, (later Sir) Peter Masefield, and named *Enterprise*, for the England-New Zealand Air Race of 1953. It covered the 12,500 mile course in 40 hr 45 min and was first in the transport aircraft class. BEA began the world's first sustained propeller-turbine airline service with the Viscount Type 701 Discovery class on 17 April 1953 and eventually acquired seventy-two Viscounts.

The 44-passenger Vickers Viscount 700 series production line at the Hurn (Bournemouth) plant with the Type 757 for Trans-Canada Air Lines (TCA) in the foreground. TCA/Air Canada eventually bought 51 Viscounts which were specially adapted for operation in the harsh Canadian winter conditions. Of the 444 Viscounts built (including prototypes), 279 were built at Hurn.

Production of the stretched (57/65-passenger) Vickers Viscount 800/810 series at Weybridge, the first of which, the Type 802 for BEA, entered service on 18 February 1957. During that year, the Weybridge and Hurn factories together delivered Viscounts at an average rate of one aircraft every three working days.

A.W.E. (Charlie) Houghton, who skillfully masterminded the complex, high-rate, customised Vickers Viscount production programme, and those of its successors, sitting alongside one of the Viscount's distinctive large elliptical (26 in by 19 in) passenger windows.

The elliptical 'structurally-neutral hole' concept was applied to the door, window, emergency-exit and pilot's canopy cut-outs in the Viscount cabin. This door shape was replaced by a wide rectangular one on the Viscount Type 802 for BEA to enable the passage of triple-seat units for rapid interior conversion and rearrangement and it continued to be used in a narrower form on all subsequent Viscount 800/810 series aircraft.

The Viscount Type 813 ZS-CDT, the first of a fleet of seven operated by Suid Afrikaanse Lugdiens (South African Airways). The total of 438 Viscounts originally sold to 60 operators in 40 countries (more than two-thirds for export and of which 147 were to North America) included 48 scheduled airlines, 5 governments and 7 private operators. British World Airlines – née British Air Ferries (BAF) – of Southend bought a large number of ex-BEA Viscount Type 806 and of which a handful will continue to operate in freight and mail service into the new millennium, while 'Viscount *Stephen Piercey*' G-APIM in BAF colours is preserved at its original home at Weybridge in the Brooklands Museum.

The Vickers Viscount Type 810 G-AOYV development aircraft, painted in the colours of Continental Airlines of the USA, the first customer of the type, with fore and aft flight test instrumentation antennae and being used for de-icing tests on the fin of the succeeding Vickers Vanguard turboprop airliner.

The prototype Vickers Valiant Type 660 WB210, the first of the Royal Air Force's much-vaunted four-jet V-bomber force, designed to Air Ministry Specification B.9/48. It was first flown by 'Mutt' Summers, Vickers CTP with 'Jock' Bryce as his co-pilot, from the grass airfield at Wisley on 18 May 1951, repeating, with much greater significance, the name of the Vickers Type 131 single-engined military tractor biplane of 1931. The rapid passage of the Valiant through design and production to operational service in September 1955 under the commanding leadership of George Edwards, exemplified 'programme management' and 'added value' par excellence long before these terms assumed the currency and status which they have today.

The Vickers Valiant Type 758 B(K)Mk.I XD823, resplendent in the white anti-flash finish carried for most of the Type's service career. Valiants saw action in Operation Musketeer during the Suez Campaign in October 1956 and thus became the first post-war four-engined jet bomber to be used in anger. The Valiant was also used to test Britain's first Blue Danube A-bomb in Operation Buffalo in Australia in September 1955. On 15 May 1957, Valiant XD818 dropped Britain's first H-bomb in Operation Grapple at Christmas Island in the Pacific and is now the sole surviving complete Valiant in preservation at the RAF Museum at Hendon. The Valiant also achieved high placings in the US Strategic Air Command's bombing competitions, Operations Long Shot and Iron Horse, in 1958 and 1959 respectively.

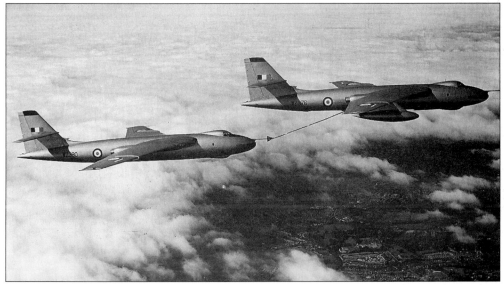

In-flight 'hose-and-drogue' refuelling greatly extended the operational radius of the Vickers Valiant, the trials being conducted from Boscombe Down using Valiant Type 710 B(PR)KMk.Is WZ390 (left) and WZ 376 (right). Logging numerous time/distance records in the process, the Valiant effectively pioneered this force-enhancing procedure for use by large jet aircraft in the Royal Air Force – notably with the RAF VC10 of today – just as its predecessors had done in the biplane era of the 1920s and 1930s.

The single Vickers Valiant Type 673 BMk.2 Pathfinder WJ954 (known as The Black Bomber because of its black night finish) with the distinguishing external features of an extended forward fuselage to accommodate the extra role equipment, and underslung Whitcomb Body type pods on the wing trailing edges, into which a new four-wheel bogie undercarriage retracted rearwards instead of sideways into the main wing structure. Ironically, this version would have been the solution to the low-level role to which the Valiant was put in 1963, but for which it had not been designed, the resulting fatigue damage leading to the entire fleet being withdrawn and scrapped in 1964. A total of 107 Valiants were built, including prototypes.

The prototype Vickers Vanguard Type 950 G-AOYW lifting off the Brooklands runway on its first flight on 20 January 1959. Designed to a BEA specification as a second-generation, low-cost, domestic and regional turboprop to follow the Viscount and with space to allow the entire payload to be accommodated on either the upper (passenger) or lower (cargo) decks, the Vanguard also ushered in large-scale structural machining and integrally-sealed 'wet' wings, together with an important new airframe anti-corrosion protection process, both of which were fully-exploited in the succeeding aircraft types built at Weybridge.

Gabe 'Jock' Bryce, Vickers Chief Test Pilot, with Brian Trubshaw, his Assistant, at Brooklands just prior to the first flight of the prototype Vickers Vanguard G-AOYW at Brooklands. Both had originally joined Vickers from the King's Flight. Bryce had succeeded Mutt Summers in 1951 and later became CTP of the British Aircraft Corporation. Trubshaw later became the celebrated British Concorde Chief Test Pilot.

The 100/140-seat Vickers Vanguard Type 951 of British European Airways exhibiting its obvious family resemblance to the highly-successful Vickers Viscount. The two chin-mounted protuberances are air-intakes for the cabin-conditioning system. BEA operated a fleet of 20 Vanguards.

A Vickers Vanguard Type 952 of Air Canada (*née* Trans-Canada Airlines) which was already operating a large fleet of Vickers Viscount turboprops. Immediately after the delivery of the first of its 23 Vanguards on 8 December 1960, the new aircraft was lined up with a Viscount and a Douglas DC-8 (long-range jet) to boast an 'all-turbine fleet' and 'the first major airline offering exclusively turbine-powered air travel on all routes – local, regional and intercontinental'. The Vanguard was described as a 'major factor in the planning of the new TCA fare structure, the lowest in North America'.

The British European Airways (BEA) cargo conversion of the capacious Vickers Vanguard of the late 1960s and early 1970s, which the airline designated Merchantman. Hunting Cargo Airlines (earlier known as Air Bridge Carriers) has recently donated the last airworthy Vanguard/Merchantman (ex-BEA G-APEP Superb) to the Brooklands Museum.

The first British Aircraft Corporation TSR-2 supersonic bomber XR219 taking off on its first flight at the Aeroplane and Armament Experimental Establishment (A&AEE) at Boscombe Down, Wiltshire, on Sunday 27 September 1964 by Roland Beaumont, the English Electric Chief Test Pilot, with Don Bowen from the Vickers-Wisley Flight Test Centre as navigator. Designed and made to specification OR339 by the Vickers-Weybridge and English Electric Aviation, Warton (Lancashire) teams in partnership, (with a significant design input from the erstwhile Vickers-Supermarine team), it had been assembled at Weybridge before transport by road to Boscombe.

The BAC TSR-2 XR219 during a test flight from Warton, Lancashire, where the flight test programme was based from 22 February 1965. The cancellation of the TSR-2 programme was announced on 6 April 1965 during the Budget speech of the new Labour Government – when XR219 was retained (grounded) at Warton until 14 August 1966 before being sent to the Shoeburyness, Essex, fire-test range. All but two of the other TSR-2 airframes were scrapped. However, the second, XR220, is now exhibited at the RAF Cosford Museum and the fourth, XR222, at the Imperial War Museum at Duxford, Cambridgeshire.

A model impression of the ambitious Vickers V1000 four-jet intercontinental transport derived from the Valiant V-bomber but cancelled in November 1955 only six months before it was due to fly. A contract had been placed for six production V1000 aircraft for RAF Transport Command and the proposed VC7 civil version included full trans-Atlantic range, fully power-operated flying controls and the first example of six-abreast passenger seating. The V1000 was also intended to act as a radio countermeasures (RCM) decoy with the same radar signature as the Valiant.

The fuselage of the first Vickers V1000 jet transport nearing completion at the Wisley flight test centre (with one wing also at an advanced stage on the right). The Government cancellation came just a month after Pan American had placed the launching order for the Boeing 707 and in the same month that it and United Airlines also placed the launching orders for the Douglas DC-8 four-engined jetliners.

The prototype Vickers VC10 Type 1100 G-ARTA rear-engined intercontinental jetliner in BOAC colours taking-off on its maiden flight on 29 June 1962 in the hands of 'Jock' Bryce and Brian Trubshaw from the 3,750 ft runway at Brooklands where it was designed and made. Vickers had originally tried a rear-engined jet installation on the Whittle-Wellington conversion in 1942 and again in 1951 on its SP2 military short-range expendable bomber project, for which the engines were mounted on the tips of the aft-mounted fins.

The 115-seat Vickers VC10 G-ARVB, the second of the fleet of 12 Standard VC10 for British Overseas Airways Corporation and of the type which had been specifically designed for operation on the airline's Medium-Range Empire (MRE) routes with their short and difficult, tropically-located, airfields. This resulted in the clean, high-lift wing and the use of the four rear-mounted Rolls-Royce Conways, the world's first operational by-pass jet engine. The near-silent passenger ride and smooth and slow landing performance of the VC10 proved to be extremely popular with passengers everywhere it operated. The VC10 was also used for pioneering automatic landing development.

The first mixed passenger/cargo conversion of the Vickers VC10 G-ASIW for British United Airways (BUA), then run by the flamboyant (later Sir) Freddie Laker and with which he launched his VC10 East and Central African service from the 1964 SBAC Farnborough Air Show, after ceremoniously loading a Rolls-Royce motor car to symbolise the 'Britishness' of the whole operation. BUA operated two VC10 Type 1103 – of which the second, G-ASIX, was later acquired by the Sultan of Oman and used as his personalised transport for thirteen years before he donated it to the Brooklands Museum in 1987. Ghana Airways also bought three of these cargo-convertible aircraft (Type 1102).

The first military VC10 Type 1106 C.Mk.I XR806 multi-mission strategic jet transport (in which concept Vickers was well versed with its Valetta of nearly two decades earlier) to Air Ministry Specification C.239, for what was then Royal Air Force Transport Command. It is seen here at the time of the first delivery to the RAF in July 1966. Each of the fourteen aircraft of this type serving with No.10 Squadron RAF were named after Victoria Cross holders. With rearward-facing seats, the VC10 C.MK.I could carry up to 150 troops and their equipment up to 4,000 miles non-stop. With the BUA-type cargo door it could also be adapted for the transport of military equipment, aero-medical evacuation (78 stretcher cases) and, later by further modification, as an aerial refuelling tanker as well as receiver.

122

The 139/163-seat Super VC10 Type 1151 G-ASGA for BOAC, the first of the fleet of seventeen of the 13 ft longer version with full trans-Atlantic capability, lifting-off on its first flight from the Brooklands runway on 7 May 1964 and flown by Bryce and Trubshaw.

The ex-RAF VC10 G-AXLR being used as a flying test-bed aircraft for the Rolls-Royce RB211 high by-pass turbofan engine, replacing the two port-side RR Conway 43 engines.

The Vickers Super VC10 Type 1154 5X-UVA, the first of a fleet of five convertible aircraft for East African Airways, which was a tri-national alliance between Kenya, Uganda and Tanzania, and hence the three national flags within the insignia on the fin were arranged for each nation to have the top position successively on the first three aircraft, with each also registered in the corresponding country, ie. 5X-UVA, 5H-MMT and 5Y-ADA respectively. The fourth and fifth – 5H-UVJ and 5H-MOG – were registered in Uganda and Tanzania respectively.

Royal Air Force VC10s provide air-to-air refuelling support to British Forces and their NATO partners from the Brize Norton, Oxfordshire, base. Number 10 Squadron currently operates 13 VC10 C.MkIK aircraft in the strategic transport role and the recently introduced air-to-air refuelling role. Number 101 Squadron operates five VC10K.Mk2s, four K.Mk.3s and five K.Mk4s – all converted by British Aerospace at Filton (Bristol) from ex-civil airliners and carrying two wing-mounted Cobham Mk.32 refuelling pods and a centreline Mk.17B Hosereel Drum Unit (HDU). The former passenger cabin of the K.Mk2s and K.Mk3s now houses five extra fuel tanks and an 18-seat support crew compartment. The K.Mk4 is similar to the K.Mk3, although it does not have the fuselage tanks and retains a transport capability with 30 seats for passengers/support crew.

The RAF VC10 K.Mk.4 ZA149 aerial refuelling tanker aircraft in the recently-applied 'battleship grey' paint scheme.

The prototype British Aircraft Corporation BAC One-Eleven 200AB G-ASHG short-to-medium range domestic and regional twin-jet airliner (in the colours of British United, the first customer) on its maiden flight at the Hurn (Bournemouth) Airport factory on 20 August 1963. It is being flown by 'Jock' Bryce, BAC Chief Test Pilot, and Mike Lithgow, the former Chief Test Pilot of Vickers-Supermarine and now the Project Pilot for the new jet. Unfortunately, this aircraft crashed on Salisbury Plain on 22 September 1963 in a deep stall accident with the loss of Mike Lithgow, his co-pilot 'Dickie' Rymer, and the flight test crew of five. However, 232 BAC One-Elevens in successive developments were ultimately built – nine at Weybridge and the remainder at Hurn – and sold worldwide, notably to key US domestic operators before the appearance of the home-grown equivalents.

Production of Concorde nose and forward fuselages at Weybridge which, after being substantially equipped, were transferred to the British and French Concorde final assembly centres at Filton (Bristol) and Toulouse in southwest France, respectively. The rear fuselage (which was largely of machined construction, including the high double-curvature skin panels and consisted of less than a hundred main parts), the fin (also mainly of machined construction) and rudder components, were similarly built at and delivered from Weybridge.

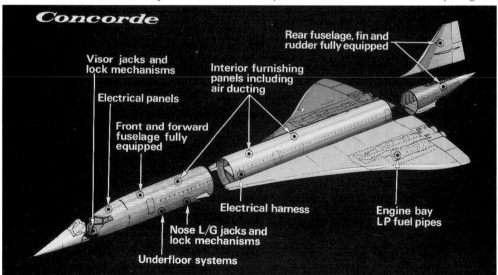

The British Aircraft Corporation (née Vickers-Armstrongs) factory at Weybridge made the largest single contribution – in design, manufacture and test – to the Anglo-French Concorde supersonic airliner programme of any of the eight manufacturing plants on either side of the Channel. The Hurn (Bournemouth) satellite also contributed the droop nose section and some of the 90 mile electrical loom harnesses. Interestingly, the last major aircraft programme at Weybridge was Anglo-French, as was the first Vickers aircraft type built at Erith, Kent, in 1908.

Envoi
Spanning and Projecting the Decades

Sir Barnes Neville Wallis CBE, FRS, HonFRAeS, FRSA, 1887-1979.

During his fifty-eight years with Vickers, after his eight-year training as a marine engineer, Barnes Wallis was at the forefront of aviation progress throughout virtually the whole history of aeronautical achievement. His often revolutionary ideas not only spanned the decades of his own generation but also projected aeronautical thinking many more decades into the future.

Before the First World War he was involved in the design of Vickers rigid airships, being responsible for the R.80, which was amongst the most beautiful ever built, and the R100, which was amongst the most successful. Between the wars he introduced the geodetic concept into aircraft design, which found successful expression in more than 12,000 wartime aircraft, and then conceived the ingenious Dambusting, Grand Slam and Tallboy outsize bombs of the Second World War. In the post-war years, he developed the swing-wing Swallow with its variable wingspan, which went on to find practical expression in swing-wing combat aircraft on both sides of the Atlantic, most notably in the European Tornado supersonic fighter/bomber aircraft of today.

As well as the key achievements already noted and illustrated, Wallis's multifarious design concepts were as diverse as an ingenious early surface-to-air cruise missile, a radio telescope in Australia, a constant-stress river bridge, the huge Stratosphere Chamber environmental test facility at Weybridge (in which many full-scale aircraft and components as well as military and industrial equipment were tested), his Universal Aircraft (quick-change passenger/cargo) with a square section pressurised cabin, and the perfecting of lighter calipers for polio victims.

Beyond all of this, his free-thinking and visionary ideas in many areas effectively projected both the aeronautical and civil engineering technologies far into the future with a trans-global cargo-carrying submarine and his All-Speed Aircraft, which could fly at speeds of up to Mach 5 or 6, avoiding extreme kinetic heating by operating in what he called the Isothermal Flight mode.

Through all of Barnes Wallis's work, his guiding principle was: 'The quality of what we do will be the deciding thing, and it is by our own quality that we shall survive'.

Acknowledgements

Now in my fiftieth year of association with Vickers and its successors at Weybridge – the British Aircraft Corporation, British Aerospace – and now the Brooklands Museum that is the proud repository of much of the rich aviation heritage of this illustrious British engineering company – it is a great privilege for me to be able to retell its aviation story.

Moreover, the corresponding privilege of knowing and working with many of the company's great leaders, designers, workpeople and customers, both at home and throughout the world, prompts me to acknowledge first my profound gratitude to them and many others like them, for the magnificent aeronautical dynasty they created and to which they bequeathed such an exciting and rewarding character.

Although I was for many years the company's custodian of many of the photographs portrayed here, I have still required the much-appreciated help of several good friends in providing appropriate pictures, information and support, and to whom I am profoundly grateful for their part in preserving such precious material, despite the vicissitudes through which it has inevitably passed during the seventy-year life of the company's aviation activity.

In this respect, I especially wish to thank Peter Boxer, Brian Wexham and Dr Mark Nicholls for access to the Vickers PLC photographic archives now carefully preserved at the Cambridge University Library, and to Hugh Scrope for his much-valued knowledge and record of Vickers aviation history. I must also thank Alan Jeffcoate and now Mike Goodall for preserving many of the photographs at Brooklands Museum which I originally helped first, the late Charles Andrews and then, Eric Morgan, to gather for their numerous, splendid publications about Vickers-Weybridge and Vickers-Supermarine aircraft for later generations and posterity; and Les Webb, Phil Jarrett, Peter Hayden and Flt Lt David Rowe of Royal Air Force Brize Norton for help with others.

I also wish to record my special gratitude to Mike Hooks, not only for originally suggesting that I should deal with both components of the Vickers aviation interests – Supermarine and Weybridge – in this commendable series but also for the loan of rare pictures from his personal collection and especially those relating to Canadian Vickers.

Dr Norman Barfield
Weybridge, Surrey